Lillian D. Wald

5.95
65p

Lillian D. Wald

Progressive Activist

Edited by Clare Coss

The Feminist Press
at The City University of New York
New York

92 91 90 89 5 4 3 2 1

Library of Congress Cataloging-in-Publication Data

Lillian Wald, progressive activist / edited by Clare Coss.
     p. cm.
   Bibliography: p.
   Contents: Lillian Wald, at home on Henry Street : a play / Clare Coss—
Letters and speeches of Lillian D. Wald.
   ISBN 1-55861-000-6
   1. Wald, Lillian D., 1867–1940—Miscellanea. 2. Women social reformers—
New York (N.Y.)—Miscellanea. 3. Public health nurses—New York (N.Y.)—
Miscellanea. I. Coss, Clare. Lillian Wald, at home on Henry Street. 1989.
II. Wald, Lillian D., 1867–1940.
HQ1439.N6L55   1989
303.4′84′092—dc20   89-32110
                                                                    CIP

This publication is made possible, in part, by public funds from the New
York State Council on the Arts.

Cover photograph: Portrait of Lillian Wald, 1919, by William V. Schevill
(1864–1951); oil on cardboard. Reproduced by permission of the National
Portrait Gallery, Smithsonian Institution, Washington, D.C. (gift of the
Visiting Nurse Service of New York).

The Henry Street Settlement emblem, which appears on the title page,
signifies "we are all one family." Lillian Wald, on her trip to the Far East in
1910, was inspired by the Chinese custom of wearing a symbol to denote
family membership. She had this one designed for the Henry Street
community.

Printed in the United States on acid-free paper by McNaughton & Gunn,
Inc.

To Joan Kelly, dear friend and mentor—
Your illuminations still light our world.

Contents

Preface

PIONEER PUBLIC HEALTH NURSE and reformer Lillian D. Wald, founder of New York City's Visiting Nurse Service and Henry Street Settlement, was a visible and influential leader of the Progressive Era. Fortified by a feminist community, sustained by alliances with like-minded women and men, from 1893 until her death in 1940 she championed causes that remain vital and immediate today. A political force to be reckoned with, she did not, however, give many clues about the private personality behind her public persona.

This book endeavors to present the scope of Wald's ideas and the principles to which she devoted her life, as well as the character of the woman behind her many achievements. It opens with a biographical introduction to outline for readers new to Wald the main events of her life, the tumultuous political context in which she lived and worked, and the personal relationships that sustained and enhanced her social and political world.

The next section features my one-character play, *Lillian Wald: At Home on Henry Street*, set on May 8, 1916, as Wald prepares to lead a peace delegation to the White House to meet with President Woodrow Wilson. Closely based on Wald's writings and actual events in her life, the play is also a creative imagining and evocation of the character of this remarkable woman.

Eight letters to and from Wald, culled from the Wald collections at the New York Public Library and Columbia University, begin the final segment of the book. Most of the letters are published here for the first time. They both illuminate a more personal side of Wald than do her public speeches, and, for students of playwriting, illustrate how primary sources were used in writing the play. The book concludes with nine speeches made by Wald. They show her most public voice passionately articulating the ideas and commitments she fought so hard to realize.

This volume focuses on the period between the founding of the Henry Street Settlement and Visiting Nurse Service in 1893 and the entrance of the United States into World War I in 1917. These years encompass a range of Wald's activism, which covered key aspects of the early-twentieth-century progressive movement for a more just society, notably public health, as addressed by Wald's campaigns for district nursing and the establishment of the Federal Children's Bureau; women's suffrage; racial justice; peace and anti-militarism; and economic security and labor issues, especially as they related to the organization of women's trade unions.

Wald was at the crest of her power nationally and internationally in 1916, the year in which the play takes place. In that year of world tension and political change, all of her accumulated street-smart, worldly-wise wealth of experience was marshaled to help keep the United States out of war. Wald risked everything for her principles and her vision of international peace. After the war, her hope for the global amity that seemed to be guaranteed by the League of Nations and the World Court was swamped by the United States's growing isolationism and xenophobia. The Red Scare of 1918 through 1921 undermined the activities of the social reformers, and the Henry Street Settlement never again enjoyed its distinctive prewar role in national politics.

This book is suitable for use in a variety of academic, theater, and other settings. For example, it can be used in courses on playwriting and biography, government, urban affairs, and history; in departments of nursing and social welfare, and in women's studies programs. Further, it is a resource for theater and acting classes, one-woman shows, women's theater companies, and organizations in the peace, health, and social work professions.

Lillian Wald's pioneering crusades for peace, public health, and human rights are of particular relevance today. As the very immune system of our vulnerable planet falters, global military expenditures continue to diminish the quality of life. Indeed all of Wald's visions need to be reconsidered. The U.S. public health structure, that she did so much to create, is now disorganized and inadequate. Even the most basic programs of maternal-child health, preventive care, environmental health, and sanitation are in disarray. We are witnessing the most serious peace-time shortage of nurses in the twentieth century. This situation poses a severe threat to the health of the public, according to the 1988 report by the Committee for the Study of the Future of Public Health of the National Academy of Sciences's Institute of Medicine.

Unlike Jane Addams of Chicago's Hull House, Lillian Wald did not write analytically about her theories and work. As a result, her generative example was temporarily lost. Wald's story joins the great restoration of women's narratives that are being rescued and are now available to enliven our discourse. Her life was full of passion and action. The more we know and understand Lillian Wald, the more we can imagine and invent the gift of giving our world a generous future.

Acknowledgments

I AM GRATEFUL to Florence Howe, co-founder and Director of The Feminist Press, who conceived the idea of a sourcebook on Lillian Wald organized around my play.

I would like to thank Woodie King, Jr., producer of the New Federal Theatre at the Henry Street Settlement, for commissioning a "celebration" of Lillian Wald and for his splendid support throughout the production of *Lillian Wald: At Home on Henry Street*. Director Bryna Wortman and I spent many exhilarating hours in script conferences. Her keen, incisive, and sensitive readings pushed me on to new discoveries in the play's development.

Many thanks go to the amiable staffs of the manuscript rooms at the New York Public Library and the Performing Arts Library at Lincoln Center; and to the congenial guardians of the manuscript collection at Columbia University. Alice Owens, Librarian of the Neighborhood Playhouse's Irene Lewisohn Library, could always put her finger on just the right document. I appreciate the comfortable facilities of the John Steinbeck Writing Room at Long Island University's Southampton campus, made available by Head Librarian Robert Gerbereux.

I also wish to express my gratitude to Daniel Kronenfeld, current Director of the Henry Street Settlement. He and his staff generously supported the production of my play, including even the loan of his treasured Chinese wall hangings for the set. Hugh McCandless of the Visiting Nurse Service's Public Relations Department and Sherry Shamansky of the VNS's National Center for Homecare Education and Research opened their resources and picture collections.

Beatrice Siegel graciously shared her impeccable research.

Her biography, *Lillian Wald of Henry Steet,* was an inspiration in itself. Over the years several friends read my play and offered salient and crystallizing commentary: Frances Clayton, Michelle Cliff, Blanche Wiesen Cook, Audre Lorde, and Adrienne Rich. Gloria I. Joseph, Alice Kessler-Harris, and Bert Silverman gave me the benefit of their insights after the first public reading at the Berkshire Forum, a New York mountain retreat for political discussion and study. An invaluable portrait of Wald was lovingly evoked in interviews with Lily Lubell and Edith Segal; Paula Trueman clarified my understanding of the place of the Neighborhood Playhouse in the Henry Street and New York theater communities.

Thanks to the Directors of the following collections for permission to quote from and publish the letters and speeches: Lillian D. Wald Papers, Rare Book and Manuscript Library, Columbia University; Lillian Wald Papers, Rare Books and Manuscripts Division, The New York Public Library, Astor, Lenox, and Tilden Foundations. All of the speeches and letters are published with the kind permission of the Visiting Nurse Service of New York.

The process of creating this sourcebook was enhanced by the excellent editorial insight and skills of Susannah Driver. Special appreciation and heartfelt thanks go to Blanche Wiesen Cook, who has been a steady support and provocative critic from the play's inception.

Chronology

1867   Born on March 10 in Cincinnati, Ohio, to Minnie Schwarz and Marcus (Max) D. Wald

1875–89   Attends Miss Cruttenden's English and French Boarding and Day School for Young Ladies and Little Girls in Rochester, New York

1891   Graduates from the New York Hospital School of Nursing on March 31

1893   Moves to Manhattan's Lower East Side with colleague Mary Brewster to offer nursing services

The founding date of two related institutions, the Henry Street Settlement and the Visiting Nurse Service of New York; in 1944 they were separated legally and each continues to thrive

1895   Moves to 265 Henry Street, a gift from Jacob Schiff, financier, her friend and mentor

1899   Helps to inaugurate a public-health nursing lecture series at Teachers College, Columbia University, which leads to the formation of the university's Department of Nursing and Health in 1910

1900   Successfully pressures the New York City Board of Education to hire Elizabeth Farrell to teach special education for children with learning disabilities and the physically handicapped, which leads to a Department for Special Education in the New York City education system in 1908

1902   Persuades the New York City Board of Education to hire the first school nurse, Lina Rogers

The nation's first playground opens in Henry Street's backyard

1903	By Henry Street's 10th anniversary Wald's nursing service embraces 18 district centers serving 4,500 patients a year through 35,035 home visits, 3,524 convalescent visits, and 28,869 first aid treatments, all privately funded
1909	Achieves a partnership between the Metropolitan Life Insurance Company and the Visiting Nurse Service in which the insurance company pays nursing care costs for its industrial policy holders; this pioneering program is followed in 1,200 municipalities
	Hosts the National Negro Conference at Henry Street, which leads to the establishment of the National Association for the Advancement of Colored People
1910	Six-month tour to Japan, China, and Russia on the Trans-Siberian Railroad with Irene Lewisohn, Yssabella Waters, and Harriet Knight
1912	Is elected first president of the National Organization of Public Health Nursing, which she helped to found
1913	The 20th anniversary celebration of the Henry Street settlement, a huge historical pageant, is the country's first street festival
	Wald now presides over 7 buildings; 92 staff nurses who make 200,000 home visits annually in the Visiting Nurse Service; and 3,000 club members and more than 25,000 active program participants in the Henry Street Settlement
1915	Co-founds and is elected president of the American Union Against Militarism
	Meets with thousands of women in Washington, D.C., to form the Woman's Peace Party
	Henry Street's Neighborhood Playhouse opens
	Publication of The House on Henry Street
1916	Leads an AUAM peace delegation with Rabbi Stephen S. Wise of the Free Synagogue, Irene Lewisohn, Crystal Eastman, labor lawyer and feminist activist, and the Reverend John Haynes Holmes, to meet with President Woodrow Wilson on May 8
	The AUAM conducts private meetings between

the United States and Mexico that serve to avert that war

With Henry Street nurses, mobilizes an all-out effort against infantile paralysis epidemic that strikes New York City

1917 After the United States declares war on the German Empire, April 6, the AUAM splits into the Civil Liberties Bureau (later renamed the American Civil Liberties Union) and the Foreign Policy Council, which Wald co-founds

1919 Represents the Federal Children's Bureau at the Conference of Red Cross Societies in Cannes, France

Attends the Woman's Peace Party's second International Conference of Women for Peace at Zurich

Is appointed adviser to the League of Nations Child Welfare Division in Paris

1920 Jacob Schiff dies

1922 Serves on the committee to free Nicola Sacco and Bartolomeo Vanzetti, two Boston anarchists convicted of murder in one of the United States's most sensational Red Scare trials

1924 Travels to the U.S.S.R. with Elizabeth Farrell to advise on public health nursing and education

1933 Retires to her Westport, Connecticut, home, "House on the Pond"

1934 Publication of *Windows on Henry Street*

Congressmen Emanuel Celler and Samuel Dickstein read speeches in Wald's honor in the House of Representatives

1937 On her 70th birthday Wald listens to a radio broadcast from Henry Street in her honor that opens with Sara Delano Roosevelt reading a letter from her son, President Franklin Delano Roosevelt

1940 Dies at Westport on September 1, at the age of 73

Lillian D. Wald

Introduction

Like the goddesses of antiquity Lillian D. Wald was given many loving and powerful titles. Nevertheless throughout her long public life this "woman of a thousand names" preferred to be known officially and simply as Head Resident of the Henry Street Settlement.

In her early days as "Nurse Wald," when she first began to serve New York's exploited and neglected immigrant population on the Lower East Side, she and colleague Mary Brewster were known as "the two young ladies who will listen." The dedicated nurses, social workers, and volunteers of the Henry Street family called her "Sister," "Lady Light," and "Dear Lady."

On the streets she became known as "She Who Must Be Obeyed" and "Boss Crocker," after the local political boss, because she admonished anyone who did not observe the new sewage and sanitation laws passed to combat disease. Alice and Irene Lewisohn, founders of Henry Street's Neighborhood Playhouse, billed her as their "Leading Lady" as they set out to achieve their "LDW" degrees in social activism. To city officials she became "That Damned Nurse Troublemaker," for her continual fight to persuade them that the well-being of each city resident was the government's responsibility. President Woodrow Wilson tried to escape the influence of her nationwide peace constituency by lamenting privately to his aide, Joseph Tumulty, that he had to see "that woman" again.[1] For the immigrant community "that woman" was forever in their hearts the true "Miss Liberty of the Lower East Side." To a Chinese-

1

American man she was "Heavenly Lady Number One." To her many progressive colleagues she was "Dear Comrade." And for the many leaders who sought the prestige and power of her support, she was "Dear Lady of Miracles, we want you to serve on our committee."

Because her private life and her public life were entwined, Wald seemed to have as many intimate friends as political allies. In their personal correspondence her friends addressed her with varied endearments: "Dear Court of Appeals," "Dearest Beloved," "Lady of the Generous Heart," "Beloved Mother of My Spirit," "Dearest Mommy," and "My Dear Joy Giver."

Lillian D. Wald was born to Minnie (Schwarz) and Max D. Wald on March 10, 1867, in Cincinnati.[2] The Schwarzes and the Walds had fled from Germany and Central Europe in the late 1840s to escape the anti-Semitism that marked that revolutionary decade. Their families settled in Cincinnati, the home of Reform Judaism, where Minnie married Max when she was sixteen. They had four children: Alfred, Julia, Lillian, and Gus. Max Wald's successful optical goods business took them to Dayton and then in 1878 to Rochester, an optical-supplies center, where they had many relatives.

As a girl, Lillian lived an assimilated, secure, comfortable life as part of Rochester's young social set. When journalist R. L. Duffus interviewed Wald in the 1930s, she recalled her father as a quiet, steady man who was taken for granted. Her mother was impulsive and unpredictable, trusting and generous to the point of having to be watched. During World War I, when Minnie Wald moved to the Henry Street Settlement House, all the residents were on guard to prevent her from giving away the entire settlement spoon by spoon, chair by chair.

As a young mother, Minnie Wald suffered from frequent headaches and Lillian ministered to her as she lay on the couch in the darkened living room. She read to her from the daily papers and, over time, George Eliot's novel *The Mill on the Floss*. When Lillian's closest sibling, Alfred, drowned in California on May 30, 1885, Minnie Wald took to her bed for months and was inconsolable for years. His death was a great loss to Lillian. For a few months she took a job (her first) as a file clerk in an uncle's firm, to get out of the house in an attempt to assuage her grief.

From the age of eight, Wald attended Miss Cruttenden's English and French Boarding and Day School for Young Ladies and Little Girls. Occasionally enrolled as a boarding student, Wald experienced her first residential community at Miss Cruttenden's. Seeing far beyond the limits of social graces and cultural refinements, Miss Cruttenden prepared and encouraged her students to go on to college. At sixteen Wald applied to Vassar, but was turned down. She attributed the rejection to her age. Whatever the actual reason, it stung her deeply and she refused to apply to college again. Her intense reaction to this event is an early indication of her temperament. Over the years, when wounded by unjust rejection or criticism, Wald responded with a cold and withholding fury. Indeed, she worked very hard not to reveal how easily she could be hurt.

Uncertain of her goals, Wald returned to Miss Cruttenden's for another two years. Wald, described by Miss Cruttenden as a young woman of "fine qualities . . . intelligence, amiability, high principles, and excitement," was restless and bored by the conventional rounds of social teas and dances and by her unchallenging work.[3]

In 1888 her sister, Julia, married Charles P. Barry, heir of a wealthy Irish family, owners of the largest seed wholesaler and nursery in Rochester. During Julia's difficult first pregnancy she required a nurse, a fact that was to change Lillian's life. As she accompanied the crisply uniformed nurse to her sister's home, Wald quizzed her on her work as an independent professional woman and her nursing school training in New York City. Wald was enthralled and inspired by the nurse's warm, efficient, caring approach to her duties.

Permission from her parents hard won, Wald eagerly applied to the New York Hospital School of Nursing. In her application she wrote:

My life hitherto has been—I presume—a type of modern American young womanhood, days devoted to society, study and housekeeping duties, such as practical mothers consider essential to a daughter's education. This does not satisfy me now. I feel the need of serious, definite work, a need perhaps more apparent since the desire to become a professional nurse has had birth.[4]

Wald refuted her family's predictions that their impulsive, free-spirited daughter would not be able to withstand the discipline demanded of a nurse in training. She entered nursing school on August 20, 1889, and, guided by Director of Nursing Education Irene H. Sutliffe, a wise woman with humor, compassion, and respect for youthful enthusiasm, Wald completed the program in a year and a half.

Nothing she experienced during that initial journey into the world of the sisterhood of nursing prepared Wald for what she saw during her first tour of duty as a staff nurse at the New York Juvenile Asylum on West 176th Street in Manhattan. Not interested in employment as a private-duty nurse, Wald thought tending to the health of children in a city institution would be useful, challenging, and fulfilling. But she found the abusive treatment of the thousand children there—some orphaned, some abandoned, others charged with criminal offenses—cruel and horrifying. The children's work-training program was a mockery of education and their living conditions were forbidding. Wald became an advocate for individual youngsters, including one boy whose tooth was about to be extracted by the asylum dentist. She insisted that he examine the tooth first, and threatened to take the child to her own dentist. Whereupon the tooth was saved.

After a year Wald quit the asylum, outraged and disillusioned by her introduction to institutionalized poverty and powerlessness. Determined to find a vocation open to women that would help to advance justice and dignity for children and all the disenfranchised, in the fall of 1892 she enrolled at the Woman's Medical College in New York City, founded by Elizabeth Blackwell, the first woman in the United States to become a doctor. For Wald the brutality of the asylum was compounded by the doctors' contemptuous treatment of the nurses. She thought that with a medical degree, she could more independently and more effectively influence public policy and civic reform.

While attending the Woman's Medical College, she enthusiastically volunteered to teach a weekly home-nursing class for immigrant women on Manhattan's Lower East Side, part of a program sponsored by philanthropist Betty Loeb. Her meetings with these persevering and heroic women turned into a crash course for herself on the daily miseries and devastating long-term effects of the great economic depression of 1893. One morning the daughter of one of her students rushed Wald to her home, through back streets and alleys, to save her hemorrhaging mother. That step across the dark threshold of the first tenement she ever saw filled Wald with a call to service. She decided "within half an hour to live on the East Side" and care for people in need directly, in their neighborhoods and in their homes.[5]

She quit medical college and, with nursing school classmate Mary Brewster, rented a fifth-floor walkup on Jefferson Street. With financial support from Betty Loeb and her son-in-law, international banker Jacob Schiff, Wald and Brewster lived in the neighborhood as nurses, identified themselves with their neighbors socially, and contributed "our sense of citizenship to what seems an alien group in a so-called democratic community."[6]

Their reputation and influence expanded rapidly beyond the immediate neighborhood. In 1895 Jacob Schiff generously donated a red-brick Georgian home at 265 Henry Street, which was officially established as the Nurses' Settlement and later known as the Henry Street Settlement and Visiting Nurse Service. Wald and Brewster provided professional care in the home at low or no cost to countless patients who otherwise would have been completely neglected. They also offered each family they visited information on health, education, sanitation, and disease prevention.

Lillian Wald attracted a powerful group of great nurse pioneers to work at the settlement. Within a short time there were eleven residents at Henry Street. Over the years they advanced dignity for the profession as well as fair pay, recognition, honor, and independence for nurses. One of the first to join "the family," as they called themselves, was the high-spirited nurse leader, feminist, educator, suffragist, and union organizer Lavinia Dock. Former superintendent of the Johns Hopkins University School of Nursing and nine years older than Wald, "Dockie" became Wald's mentor.

Family member Adelaide Nutting was also a suffragist and innovator in nursing education. She became the chair of the Department of Nursing and Health at Teachers College, Columbia University, in 1910, a department that Wald worked tirelessly to establish and endow.

Also part of Wald's household were nurse leaders Anne Goodrich, Director of Nurses for the settlement; Lina Rogers, head of the first public school nursing service in the world; and Yssabella Waters, graduate of The Johns Hopkins School of Nursing, among others.

Members of the "laity," as non-nurses in Wald's Henry Street community were called, included Helen McDowall and Florence Kelley. The wealthy daughter of a Union Army general, McDowall, known as "Tante Helene," bought the house behind 265 Henry Street and offered art classes, club meetings, musicals, and theatricals there. Florence Kelley was a fiery and brilliant attorney, social activist, socialist, and general secretary of the National Consumers' League. Kelley and Wald set up a New York Child Labor Committee, and together they initiated what was to become the Federal Children's Bureau.

Jane Addams, founder of Chicago's Hull House, was a trusted political ally with whom Wald frequently traveled and worked. For decades they spent most summers together, traveling with other friends or staying at Addams's summer house high above Hull's Cove in Bar Harbor, Maine.

This community of women inspired and encouraged one another. Their animated exchanges helped to develop Wald's social conscience and deepened her involvement in the areas of health care, employment, housing, immigration, trade unions, children's rights, city government, education, peace, racial justice, civil liberties, recreation, and culture.

The number of committees and causes that claimed Wald's active commitment is staggering. She took each one seriously and would not serve unless she could personally attend meetings and make her voice heard. This was all in addition to her major responsibilities as founder and head of the Visiting Nurse Service and the Henry Street Settlement and its many branches, camps, and clinics. The House on Henry Street spearheaded a national and international movement for independent public health nursing.

The settlement became a center of community living that inspired scores of activists—women and men dedicated to a humane and caring future, all of whom turned to Henry Street for

6

direction and for political and emotional support. Once, at the opera during a rare evening off, Wald was distracted by the thought that she was the cause of so many affluent and privileged young people who had decided to sacrifice the regular course of their lives in order to dedicate themselves to the work of the settlement. "The thought was so bitter that I had to get up and go out into the lobby. It was terrible while it lasted. Then I thought, they were, after all, adults, and had made their own choice. I felt better and went back to hear the last act."[7]

There were many independent and occasionally conflicting personalities within the large and complex community that centered around Wald. Personally she was closer to some than to others. In addition to her family of "steadies," as the nurses who lived at Henry Street called themselves, many of the young women and men who came to work at the settlement were devoted to Wald and adopted her as their mother surrogate—most notably, Alice and Irene Lewisohn. In 1904 their father, Leonard Lewisohn, one of Wald's dedicated backers, brought his daughters to her for solace when their mother died. Alice Lewisohn recalled her first visit:

Could this be Miss Wald? This crisp blue figure, the gay voice, welcoming smile, cordial gesture, handsome face ovaled by dark hair? Yes. She was vital, real, exuberant, and, most overwhelming of all, joyous. . . .

The Leading Lady conducted us downstairs and into the dining room, the others following. . . . Bubbling spirits sparred back and forth across the table, and, at its head, delving into a deep Chinese bowl, the Lovely Leading Lady turned, mixed and dressed crisp green lettuce leaves. . . .[8]

After dinner Alice Lewisohn caught her first glimpse of Lillian Wald at home on Henry Street for a "quiet" evening with friends. "Her presence was felt here, there, everywhere, she herself the first to hear a knock at the front door and to respond to an incoherent stumbling appeal for a nurse." Then there was a "delegation of push-cart vendors, bearded . . . gaunt and timid" who needed advice regarding a new law that threatened their trade. Then a young woman writer called wanting and expecting instant information for her article on local conditions. All the while "a university student patiently waited his turn to confer about a labor dispute."⁹

The way to be close to Lillian Wald was to create programs she would find indispensable to the Henry Street community. The Lewisohn sisters taught classes in dance and theater, and in 1913 organized the settlement clubs to present New York City's first street festival in celebration of Henry Street's twentieth anniversary. A cast of thousands honored the culture and history of diverse ethnic and racial groups from all over the city, beginning with a portrayal of the Manhatta Indians. In 1915 the Lewisohns founded the settlement's Neighborhood Playhouse Theatre. Internationally acclaimed, the Neighborhood Playhouse became a living monument to the best and most innovative in theater, music, and dance.

There were also women in her life with whom Wald shared her most private and intimate moments. Her correspondence with Mabel Hyde Kittredge, for example, is replete with passages of ardor and longing. One evening past midnight, Kittredge wrote:

> I am writing in a low necked gown with roses in my hair and rings on my fingers. It seems to represent a world where hearts are never laden. And yet the real thing to me as I sit here now is your letter and the little enclosed notes. The dinner and gaiety I have just left seem already far away. I will see you tomorrow night but not what I call seeing you. And I don't quite dare risk your being up at this hour.

And another evening, Kittredge wrote:

> But what business has a great grown woman like myself to sit up in her nightclothes and write nothings. . . . I am getting altogether too close to you Lady Wald—or is it . . . all those doors that you have pushed open for me? Half open—dear—just half open. . . . I can feel your arms around me as you say I really must go.¹⁰

For several years Wald reserved a special place in her heart for Mabel Hyde Kittredge. The daughter of a leading New York minister, Kittredge was a generous donor to Henry Street. She moved from her Park Avenue home to reside temporarily at the settlement early in the 1900s. Something of an anomaly in Wald's life, Kittredge was witty and arrogant. She was charmed by Wald, but she was not at ease at Henry Street and was not always in tune with the political purposes of her co-workers. An elitist and fundamentally class-bound, her major interest was domestic science. For example, she directed the Association of Practical Housekeeping Centers, which aimed to Americanize and whitewash immigrant culture. Although Wald agreed with the goal of assimilation, she had a greater respect for and celebrated the cultural heritage of her constituency, believing it should not be lost. Despite their disagreements, Kittredge always supported Wald's activities and together they introduced the New York City free school-lunch program.

Strong-willed and seductive "Kitt" ultimately wanted more of Wald's time than Wald wanted to give. Their relationship was for several years Wald's most intense enthusiasm, but her primary commitment was always to Henry Street while Kitt hoped for exclusivity. Although the intensity of their relationship could not endure their different needs, they remained friends. In 1915 Kitt represented Henry Street at the International Peace Conference at the Hague.

For a time lawyer Helen Arthur succeeded Kittredge in Wald's affections. Flamboyantly generous, her expenses frequently exceeded her income. Wald, always concerned as much with the private details of her friends' lives as with the great principles of reform politics, monitored Arthur's finances and put her on an allowance.

Wald and Arthur spent part of August and September of 1906 on vacation in the country. In a letter dated January 4, 1907, Arthur reminisced about that privileged time they had shared:

> I've put you—the dear old you—in your silver frame on my desk and close to me when I write and I shoved my decanter and cigarette case to the other side—If I had you, the real you instead of one ten thousandth part of you I might shove the unworthy things way off—summertime has spoiled the Judge [Wald's nickname for

Arthur] who longs to get back to your comfortable lap and the delights of kicking her pajamaed legs in peace and comfort instead of being solicitously hustled from your room at ten o'clock.

On January 30, 1907, Arthur wrote to Wald:

"Dearest,"
Little by little there is being borne in upon me, the presumption of my love for you, the selfishness of its demands, the triviality of its complaints—and more slowly still, is coming the realization of what it ought to bring to you and what I mean it shall.[11]

Lily Lubell, a lead performer at the Neighborhood Playhouse, remembered Arthur as "quite a pixie, bright as a whistle, and a little devilish, too."[12] She often cross-dressed in high collars and ties, which Wald found charming. Arthur became the business manager of the Neighborhood Playhouse shortly after its founding in 1915. She worked closely with Agnes Morgan, its artistic director. According to Paula Trueman, a lead dancer and actor with the Neighborhood Playhouse, Agnes Morgan and Helen Arthur "were a lesbian couple. Just everyone knew."[13]

Wald, who delighted in the happiness of her friends, apparently never wanted for herself or encouraged an exclusive or permanent partnership, such as Jane Addams shared with Mary Rozet Smith. While her letters to Kittredge and Arthur have been lost, we do know she inspired flirtatious longings and passionate pleadings. However much she encouraged these relationships, she remained in the end forever elusive. She preferred personal independence, which allowed her to move quickly, travel freely, and act boldly.

For Lillian Wald, work and love were inextricably bound. Her admirers were continually drawn into her dazzling orbit of contained magnetic energy and clearheaded sense of purpose. Similarly, her impassioned political convictions, as well as her actions and emotions, were fueled and fired, protected and enhanced, by the community of women who comprised her chosen Henry Street family.

The Henry Street Settlement, and all of Wald's political and nursing projects, depended entirely on private contributions. It was a reflection of her intelligence and radiant personality that a wide range of people gave her the financial support she needed. Among the most generous contributors were the leading politicians and philanthropists of the fin de siècle. Over the years Wald was able to maintain a loyal and caring relationship with financier Jacob Schiff, her primary sponsor. Wald's affiliation with Schiff and his wife, Therese, survived many turbulent disagreements and political strains. Indeed Wald had to walk a diplomatic tightrope with all of her major sponsors. Her correspondence with Schiff, from her first daily reports, which accounted for each penny spent in 1893, to her last concerned letters before his death in 1920, document a close and loving friendship based on mutual respect between two tough-minded political partners.

Other major contributors to the ever-expanding needs of Henry Street included Henry Morgenthau, who became Secretary of the Treasury under FDR, and his wife, Elinor, who was particularly generous to the Neighborhood Playhouse; the banker Solomon Loeb and his wife, Betty, who with Schiff first sponsored Wald and Mary Brewster in 1893; Caroline O'Day, antiwar activist, artist, philanthropist, member of Congress from 1935 to her untimely death in 1943; and many philanthropist families including the Lehmans, Cranes, McCormicks, Belmonts, and Warburgs.

Lillian Wald sailed into every room, whether for dinner at a benefactor's fund-raiser or to bring support into the poorest home, with the same dignity and warmth and purpose. It was not a cliché when Wald said so often, "The whole world is my neighborhood."

She was repelled by the rigid segregation and race cruelty that prevailed throughout her lifetime. When New York City's law prohibited integrated public meetings, Wald offered Henry Street, in 1909, for the National Negro Conference that led to the creation of the National Association for the Advancement of Colored People.

She worked with Mary White Ovington, one of the founders of the NAACP, to bring a controversial production of Angelina Weld Grimké's play, *Rachel*, to the Neighborhood Playhouse in 1917. Grimké was the black grandniece of white abolitionist leaders Sarah and Angelina Grimké. In this play she followed in their famous tradition: *Rachel* was an appeal to white women for compassion and action against the evils of race hatred and lynchings. It was the first time a theater in the United States presented a play by a black author with a black cast before an integrated audience.

In 1914 Wald became an ardent peace activist. The issue of world peace was to become her most controversial commitment and would cause her to lose sponsors as never before. In 1916 she co-founded and presided over the American Union Against Militarism, created to keep America neutral and out of Europe's war. In its first brochure, the AUAM pleaded for negotiations between warring nations, contending that war would destroy everything that decades of social reform had built. In this organization she worked with the leaders of the most radical wing of the reform movement, especially socialists like feminist attorney Crystal Eastman and her brother Max who then edited *The Masses*, a journal of social protest.

Her political allies in the AUAM also included Emily Greene Balch, professor of economics at Wellesley College; Rabbi Stephen S. Wise of the Free Synagogue; Paul Kellogg, editor of the radical social-work journal *The Survey*; socialist-feminist, and popular novelist and playwright Zona Gale; progressive minister John Haynes Holmes; and Roger Baldwin, co-founder, with Crystal Eastman and others, of the American Civil Liberties Union, originally called the Civil Liberties Bureau, a branch of the AUAM.

On April 6, 1917, the United States declared war on the German Empire. The AUAM shifted its emphasis to keeping democracy alive in wartime and to guaranteeing civil liberties in the face of the virulent repression intensified by the Espionage Act of June 1917 and, later, the Sedition Act of May 1918.

Wald favored continued negotiation with Wilson's administration for a democratic postwar peace settlement, and helped to found the Foreign Policy Association. Eventually, tactical differences within the AUAM became irreconcilable, and Wald resigned as president in September 1917. After the war, Wald continued her peace work with the Foreign Policy Association, which sought to substitute world law for world war. She hoped that the League of Nations she and Jane Addams had worked vigorously for would prevent another war.

Her antiwar activities and her association with the Woman's Peace Party and the AUAM caused her to be named in the first "Red Scare" list of sixty-two American men and women, "Who's Who in Pacifism," compiled by the U.S. Military Intelligence Bureau and published in the press and presented to a Senate Judiciary Committee. All those identified were accused of leading pro-German pacifist movements prior to the U.S. entry into the war. Wald's name, along with that of Jane Addams and all their associates, also appeared in a list of "undesirable citizens" issued by the Overman Committee, the 1919 congressional committee set up to investigate "un-Americans." Also in 1919, New York State's Lusk Committee investigated "radicalism" in settlement houses and schools. In 1921 Lillian Wald and Jane Addams were singled out in the Lusk Report as two women "anxious to bring about the overthrow of the government and establish in this country a soviet government on the same lines as in Russia."

At first those named felt honored by the good company in which they were placed. Wald commented to Dock on the postwar hysterics and the sponsors who withdrew from Henry Street: "Poor things. I am sorry for them. They are so scared." She found the charges against her "foolish since after all, counting the large and wide, I am at least one insurance against unreasonable revolution in New York."[14] But everyone knew that the lists and committees were sobering signs, harbingers of a deepening political discord.

Despite the Red-baiting climate that mushroomed in the United States after the Russian Revolution of 1917, Lillian Wald continued to play a leading role in support of an amazing variety of issues, including: women's suffrage; the Visiting Nurse Service mobilization in New York City to fight the 1918 Spanish influenza epidemic; the Woman's Peace Party (renamed the Women's International League for Peace and Freedom, in 1921); anti–Ku Klux Klan organizations; the Federal Children's Bureau; the American League to Abolish Capital Punishment; the American Anti-Imperialist League for Independence of the Philippines from the U.S.; the movement to reestablish diplomatic relations with the Soviet Union (not achieved until 1933); and the effort to get the United States to join the World Court (not achieved until after World War II).

Periodically after 1912 Wald suffered from exhaustion and occasionally withdrew from all activity to her Westport, Connecticut "House on the Pond." In 1925, vacationing with Jane Addams and Mary Rozet Smith in Mexico, she became extremely ill and on her return to the United States had a hysterectomy and an appendectomy. She never fully recovered her strength.

When in 1933 Franklin Delano Roosevelt and Wald's friend Eleanor Roosevelt entered the White House, she wrote that her years of struggle had been fulfilled. There was now, she believed, an administration that officially defined as national priorities the issues to which she had dedicated her life.

Lillian Wald died of a cerebral hemorrhage at her home in Westport on September 1, 1940, after a long illness. Her friend Paul Kellogg wrote in his eulogy, printed in the *New York Times* on September 3:

> Let me single out one strand in Miss Wald's leadership that sprang from her insight into human relations, and has much to give us today. Every nation in Europe was represented among the people that found the way to the house on Henry Street. Against this background, twenty-five years ago, at the very outset of the World War, she risked much to take the chairmanship of the AUAM. Out of it came the American Civil Liberties Union. It was one of the roots of the Foreign Policy Association. There was a stage when Miss Wald, herself, helped tellingly in staving off war with Mexico. She met the temper of the times with clarity and courage. Her constructive bent counted then and leaves her living heritage now.

Rabbi Stephen S. Wise led a memorial service at the Neighborhood Playhouse immediately after her death. Several months later 2,500 friends gathered at New York's Carnegie Hall for a memorial service led by Mayor La Guardia. Messages from the president, the governor, and her Henry Street neighbors celebrated the fullness of a life that had combined adventure, love, humor, and activism.

Lillian D. Wald's courage, vision, and integrity enabled her to imagine what had not existed before. Her own need of and reliance on community grew out of her realization that no individual acting alone can attain the power of people who are organized and united in a common goal. Always engaged, always a crusader for caring human values, her life was a model of achievement. The creative institutions she built still flourish and continue to grow and adapt in order to meet the challenges of each new generation.

Notes

1. For Wilson's attitude toward Lillian Wald and the antimilitarists, see Blanche Wiesen Cook, "Woodrow Wilson and the Anti-Militarists, 1914-1917" (Ph.D. diss., Johns Hopkins University, 1970).

2. "Wahl" was the original family name and then "de Wald." In the United States, Max Wald adopted the middle initial "D" for himself and for each child.

3. Student records, May 1899, Cornell University–New York Hospital School of Nursing, Medical Archives, The New York Hospital–Cornell Medical Center.

4. Ibid., p. 4.

5. Lillian D. Wald, *House on Henry Street* (New York: Henry Holt, 1915), p. 7.

6. R. L. Duffus, *Lillian Wald, Neighbor and Crusader* (New York: Macmillan, 1938), p. 35.

7. Ibid., p. 91.

8. Alice Lewisohn Crowley, *The Neighborhood Playhouse* (New York: Theatre Arts Books, 1959), pp. 5-6.

9. Ibid.

10. Mabel Hyde Kittredge to Wald, undated letter [1904-1906?]. All Kittredge's letters are undated, except for captions such as; "Very late Monday night or rather early Tuesday." Lillian D. Wald Papers, Rare Book and Manuscript Library, Columbia University Libraries.

11. Helen Arthur to Wald, Wald Papers, Columbia University, Box 14.

12. Author's interview with Lily Lubell, May 19, 1985.

13. Author's interview with Paula Trueman, May 19, 1985.

14. Duffus, *Lillian Wald*, p. 212.

I. *Lillian Wald: At Home on Henry Street*

Writing the Play

In the early 1970s, while working on a graduate degree in Social Work at the State University of New York at Stony Brook, I wrote a paper on Lillian D. Wald for a History of Social Welfare course. Her commitment to culture and justice and her charismatic energy, resourcefulness, and ingenuity compelled me to learn more about her.

During the resurgence of the feminist movement in the 1970s, I was co-artistic director of the Women's Experimental Theater and a lecturer in Hunter College's theater department in New York City. As I commuted from classroom to theater to classroom, vivid scenes of Wald, on stage, played over and over in my mind. Sometimes she would plead: "Mother, please, I want to be a nurse, I want to be out in the world. Please let me go." Or belt out a song: "Henry Street! Henry Street!" Or win over a sponsor: "But it is a *privilege* to serve!" Or address the crowd at Carnegie Hall under a huge banner, DEMOCRACY VS. MILITARISM: "Fear has dethroned reason and people are seeing things at night."

The seed had been planted. I knew it would be a challenge to write a political play about a great American leader, a woman who would not be portrayed as women usually are on stage: insane, a suicide, a rape victim, a sex object, a man hater, or a fluff.

After graduating I called a friend, Woodie King, Jr., producer of the New Federal Theatre of Henry Street's Louis Abrons Center of the Arts, and told him, "If you ever want a play about Lillian Wald, I'm ready." His reply was to commission a

one-character play on Wald for the 1986 centennial of the Settlement House Movement in the United States, to be staged at
the original Neighborhood Playhouse on Grand Street, now the
New Federal Theatre.

In 1935 Wald wrote to a friend, "I hope to goodness nobody
will ever write my biography—I would 'hant' them if they
did." I always enter into dialogues with my characters and
"haunt" me she did. I complained to her: "If only you had
been a revolutionary instead of a reformer, all the same problems might not still be facing us today." We tussled, and she
led me to her 1919 letter calling attacks on aliens "a kind of
smokescreen to deflect the attentions from the real conflict,
that between capital and labor." I insisted: "But you chose to
work within the system." She patiently explained that until we
have a more perfect world, each day of our lives is about "the
struggle." As privileged people we each are free to choose how
we are engaged in that struggle.

Wald's call to reverse the military buildup and stop the in-
vention of ever more deadly weapons at the time of World War
I caught my attention. She and her compatriots sincerely believed it was still possible to prevent public funds from being
stolen away from education, health care, and housing in order
to fatten the coffers of the munitions makers. To turn the world
away from war, she risked everything.

The conflict between living by her principles and keeping
Henry Street solvent emerged as the cutting edge of the play.
I realized the one person she would not want to cause a break
with would be Jacob Schiff, her primary benefactor. Wald's un-
derlying struggle in the play is how to justify her Washington,
D.C., peace mission to Schiff without jeopardizing his essential
financial and personal support.

In 1916 Wald's national and international reputation, power,
and influence were at their height. May 8, 1916, seemed to
me the perfect time to capture Wald: the moment in history
that took her to President Wilson's White House. Once I
had decided on the time, setting, theme, and conflict for
the play, I savored the documents and writings that related
to that vision. I took copious notes—words, phrases, longer
sections, to capture a feeling and flavor and texture of Wald

and her associates. Most of the play is based on actual remarks, events, and interactions from Wald's life. Examples of letters that engendered particular moments of dialogue follow the play.

As I wrote the play, I imagined other scenes; for example, little Ernie Brofsky's flight up a hill, thinking he swallowed a tadpole. There was something about his beating heart, and her beating heart, and the hearts of all the soldiers—two-and-a-half million boys whose hearts had stopped beating in the first two-and-a-half years of war.

I interviewed three women who had known Lillian Wald as head resident of the settlement and in yet another of her roles, that of theater producer of Henry Street's Neighborhood Playhouse. Edith Segal, poet, dancer, and political activist, had attended Henry Street classes and fresh-air camps. The line in the closing scene, "For weeks the buildings waved like trees," is from that interview.

Paula Trueman, lead dancer and actor in the first seasons of the Neighborhood Playhouse, introduced me to Lily Lubell. "Lily replaced me as the big darling of the Playhouse, but I never held it against her. We're still friends." (The phrase "big darling of the Playhouse" also found its way into the play.)

Lily Lubell's recollections rounded out the essence of my portrait of Wald. "She would inspire you to bring out the best of yourself—an aura of goodness in you. You just felt that she was telling you something that was going to make a difference to the world. That there was so much to do to make the world a better place and we all have to get together and realize that we are all for one and one for all. She was a dream person. You could see it in her eyes, in her face, in everything about her. And she was very playful and entertaining. I used to look up at her—I was so little, she was so big. I used to take a deep breath and think oh, how lucky I am. Even now as I think of her, I could almost cry."

Lubell's sentiments echoed those of Lavinia Dock, who said of Wald: "She believed absolutely in human nature and as a result the best of it was shown to her. People just naturally turned their best natures to her scrutiny and developed what she perceived in them, when it had been dormant and unseen in them before. I remember often being greatly impressed by this inner vision that she had."[1]

How I wanted to capture this remarkable woman, and bring her to life on the sacred stage!

On October 9, 1986, the run opened at the New Federal Theatre with a gala benefit for the Henry Street Settlement. Bryna Wortman directed luminously, and Tony-award-winner Patricia Elliott played a magnetic and gallant Lillian Wald. The set was designed by Richard Harmon, lighting by Jackie Manassee, and costumes by Gail Cooper-Hecht.

Since the New Federal Theatre production, I have read the play at colleges, benefits, and conferences for nurses, social workers, and women's studies students. Her spirit and presence continue to inspire, and audiences are struck by the immediacy of the issues that propelled Wald's own activism.

Note

1. R. L. Duffus, *Lillian Wald, Neighbor and Crusader* (New York: Macmillan, 1938), p. 347.

Lillian Wald:
At Home on Henry Street

Lillian Wald, founder of the Henry Street Settlement House, has a charismatic, persuasive quality. She is strong-willed but tender. Her charm radiates a warmth that could embrace the whole world.

She is wearing a dusty-rose silk kimono and pearl gray leather slippers. The kimono was a gift from the Kyoto Peace Society.

(LILLIAN WALD *steals into her office, softly closing the door behind her.*)
All the ladies of the Henry Street Settlement House—sound asleep. Sleep is an interruption. I manage four hours' sleep a night, and play tricks with the clock to fit thirty-six hours into each day. Except once when my friends insisted: Lillian Wald, we are taking you to Italy for a nap.
(SHE *checks the day's calendar on her desk. Reads.*)
May 8, 1916. Agenda.
Five A.M. — Mountains of correspondence.
     Answer Mr. Schiff.
Six-thirty — Depart for train station; take peace petitions.
Seven — The Washington Express.
Two P.M. — The White House.
Where I am to convince President Wilson to keep the U.S. neutral and out of Europe's war. Call for a conference of neutral nations to end the war! How did I get myself into this one? I know the delegation has infinite faith in my powers of persuasion—but really, Lillian.
Not one sleeper stirred as I tiptoed through each room. I

hoped to hear a whisper, "Lillian, what's wrong?" I lay awake all night, my mind caught—pacing back and forth, back and forth, caught by the words in Mr. Schiff's letter. "Caution. Caution, my dear Lillian. The country is turning towards war. By going to Washington you endanger everything you have worked to build these past twenty-three years."

Docky and I had words last night. I wish she had awakened just now when I pulled back her goose-down comforter. So she could BREATHE. The first warm spring night Docky and I move cots out onto the back upstairs porch overlooking Bunker Hill. That's the children's name for the first playground in America. We sleep outside every night until mid-October. Like firemen. Always at the ready to jump up and out on emergency calls.

I was certain Tante Helene would awaken. Each morning she pops up at the exact moment of sunrise to move her way through a short Tai Chi exercise she learned during our stay in Peking. Last night she chided, "Dear Lady, you need your sleep like other mortals. Stay home tomorrow. Conserve your strength. A member of your delegation can speak in your stead— Reverend Holmes. Rabbi Wise is convincing. Crystal Eastman."

"Tante Helene, it is not a matter of speaking to Wilson. I must convince him it is more patriotic to live for your country than to die for it."

Tante Helene is what we call here a member of the laity. Not a nurse, but an honorary member of the sisterhood. She bought the house behind so we could openly combine backyards and have four floors for classrooms. Before Bunker Hill the children's only play spaces were the streets—littered, foul-smelling, dangerous. The first years our playground was thronged with lines waiting to get in. A schedule was designed. Baby hammocks and young mothers in the mornings; canvas swings, or scups, as the children call them, in the afternoons; and in the evenings, for adults, parties under Japanese lanterns. A young neighborhood man said as he wove the luscious old wisteria vine onto the trellis, "Miss Wald, I am thinking, this must be like the scenes of country life in English novels." The wisteria has climbed clear up to our pillared sleeping porch.

Docky and I had words last night. I can still not go to Washington. Mr. Schiff is right to question how my principles will affect the future of the Henry Street Settlement. The torture chamber of losing sponsors.

The moment my meeting with President Wilson hits tomorrow morning's front page, the phone will ring. The door knocker will pound. Irate sponsors will hurl their accusations: "Unpatriotic, Miss Wald! In good conscience we must withdraw our support from the settlement! Stay out of politics and keep to nursing. War is good for the economy."

War. All the suffering from war. I feel it in every fiber of my body, down to my very toes. I am a nurse! Pledged to save lives. Madness. Why can't people see the connection between war and poverty? We want to provide each child under the age of five with a medical exam and nursing care. As a right. *Imagination.* My favorite word in the English language. President Wilson, use your imagination.

Cold, charming, imperious Woodrow Wilson. "Miss Wald, I agree the world has gone mad. My program is preparedness. In case we are invaded—another Lusitania. As for war, my mind is still to let."

If he dares to use that expression on me again, do I dare ask him, "Who's the highest bidder for your mind? The munitions makers and all the politicians in their pockets, or the thousands of citizens who want peace"?

Yesterday Mrs. Brofsky confided, "Miss Wald, we thought we left beautiful bleeding Europe behind us." Police Captain Handy pleaded, "Miss Wald, how can a great, modern, intelligent nation become involved in war?" The reaction of our Henry Street neighbors to the fact of war is sheer bewilderment.

(Singsong slogan.)

"He Kept Us Out of War. He Kept Us Out of War." His campaign slogan.

"Miss Wald, please, endorse my drive for re-election. You and your friend Jane Addams must join our campaign."

I reminded Jane of what she had said in 1912, "Lillian, I'll swallow two battleships and no more." What a mistake that was. When you put a gun in a man's hand you give him the best argument for shooting.

Miss Addams and I are withholding our endorsement until

we are convinced the president is taking every step possible toward the conference table.

Yes. Wilson with all the might of his office has just leaned hard on Congress to pass the National Defense Act, giving the military carte blanche. For years we struggle to have school nurses. With the flick of a pen, we have military training in our schools.

Louis Rifkin first set my mind in motion to place a nurse in each school. When I first saw Louis Rifkin through an open door in a rear tenement flat, I thought, Why isn't that boy in school? His mother, with a newborn baby, was standing over a tub washing butchers' aprons. She told me the school officials barred him from the classroom since first grade because of his scaly, sore scalp. Louis, thirteen years old, was embarrassed that he couldn't read—not even the names of streets on lampposts. I examined his scalp. There was only a mild fungus disease that an ointment cleared up in no time. Louis was ecstatic. Back in school, he quickly learned how to read and catch up on all those lost years. And I quickly learned that when you see an individual suffering, you help that person out on the spot. Then you work to remove the cause.

War. Why not a Department of Peace, Mr. President, with well-paid, full-time employees? No.

Too emotional. I must drain myself of emotion. Men avert their eyes from the impassioned pleas of women. Only facts.

"Miss Wald, show me the peace support. Hire halls across the country. Collect signatures."

Here, President Wilson. Sheaves of signatures. Testimony collected by the American Union Against Militarism, the AUAM, founded right here in this room, my room, the day war was declared in Europe, August 7, 1914! We toured the country with a six-foot dinosaur to illustrate what happens when you become too heavily armed for your own good. Extinction!

Oh, tomorrow's headlines: WALD: WARNING VOICE AGAINST PREPAREDNESS! Just two years ago I marched with thousands of other women down Fifth Avenue for peace! Thousands of citizens all over the country joined in a massive call for the U.S. to lead Europe to the conference table. Peace without victory. A lasting peace. No more war to end all wars. Mr. Schiff says such a peace march today would be considered highly suspect. Unpatriotic. He is right. It would. The country has swung toward war.

Docky and I had words last night. I had asked what she thought of Mr. Schiff's warning me not to go to Washington today.

"Lillian, my dear, why waste your time appealing to the president of white American men? He even refuses to support votes for women! Yet craves your endorsement—wants your whole constituency to back him for reelection. The only salvation for politics is for women to get the vote. Join us instead. We'll chain ourselves to the White House gates, not waltz through them."

I said, "We cannot wait for women to get the vote! What is our alternative but to appeal to men holding the reins of power? Yes, I'm for the vote, but first things first! You suffragettes—"

"Suffragist. Ist. Not ette. Suffragette is a man's word denoting a diminutive female."

"I'm sorry, Docky. Suffragist. Ist. I apologize. Lavinia Dock. Please turn around. Scholar, pianist, nurse extraordinaire. My teacher—"

"You refuse to learn, Lillian, that the men in power destroy every social, every progressive reform we've dedicated our lives to."

"Docky, what good will women's votes do if we let this country become militarized? War destroys democracy."

"Wilson is not going to listen to you, Lillian. Women have to have equal political power. So we can save men from themselves."

"And where is your guarantee that most women won't vote along with their husbands?"

"Oh, dear Lady Light, I would rather be sitting on my front porch in the hills of Pennsylvania—where my greatest concern is that the cat slapped PeeWee over the ear and scratched his eyes, and the tomatoes ripen so fast no one can eat them up."

"Dear friend, chain yourself to the White House gates, and you will end up arrested and in that medieval Virginia prison again. At your age. Sixty! You will lead another hunger strike. They will brutally force-feed you. Ram a tube down your nose."

"And on your visit, Lillian, I will raise myself up and confide, 'My dear, the only salvation for politics is for women to get the vote.' "

The cat slapped PeeWee over the ear—

(Low chuckle.)

I can still see Docky, Election Day 1896, her short, roly-poly body striding furiously through the front door. "Votes for Women" banners emblazoned across her jacket and pinned to her straw hat. "We stormed the polling booth around the corner and cast our votes. Lillian, the police arrested every voting suffragist and threw them into jail, except me!" Up the stairs, stomp, stomp, stomp, and slam. This is the House of Perpetual Doors Slamming. Captain Handy came by, repentant, hat in hand. "Miss Wald, please don't be mad at me. I couldn't arrest the little doc. I just couldn't do it. She nursed my son back to health herself. I had to pull her off the paddy wagon. She was kickin', you know."

The most extraordinary nurse I know is ready to risk her life for votes for women. Have I ever put my life on the line? Docky says I've defied death from my first day down here—exposed to disease, riots, exhaustion. If I go to Washington today, I risk losing my home, my sustenance, this center that has brought light into so many lives. Especially my own.

Lavinia Dock, you have been my mainstay for over twenty years. But on this issue, dear friend—

I know, Jane Addams, you would advise me to go, wouldn't you?

Miss Addams and I were up all night on her return from the European front. Count on her for surprises. I love surprises. "Lillian, let's bake bread. When I met with Tolstoy he had me convinced that to save my soul I must bake bread for two hours each day." Once Jane returned home from the Russian steppes, Tolstoy's bread labor seemed preposterous.

But now, filled with stories of torment from the trenches, she wanted to bake bread. So we stole down to the kitchen in the middle of the night and talked and kneaded and rolled out the dough. We hardly noticed the two hours it took to rise. As we were buttering the first warm bite, Jane announced, "Lillian, Tolstoy was wrong. Baking bread will not save our souls, but it has delivered us through this night." Refreshed, without a wink of sleep, we went back upstairs to start the day.

Oh, how much younger and simpler the world seemed before August 7, 1914. Before Europe burst into flames! So much optimism—peace and utopian societies, the progressive movement Henry Street helped to build. There had been no major war in Europe since Napoleon. We genuinely believed the moral forces of humanity had reached beyond war.

Now newspapers are saturated with pictures from all across Europe glamorizing war. Women and children stand in doorways, at train stations, with white handkerchiefs, waving their men off to be slaughtered. Nurses next to their field ambulances, smiling. What the papers don't show us are nurses sewing them up before sending them back for more. It's up to women to remove the glamour from war.

At least President Wilson has agreed to have this afternoon's meeting. I had wanted to meet at dinner. Teddy Roosevelt always invited me to stay on for dinner at the White House. But tonight the Wilsons have tickets for the circus! We do have four solid hours. Will he betray us and turn it into a press conference of preparedness? No. I don't think so. He's given us the entire afternoon. To accomplish the impossible.

The impossible. Tante Helene said, "Lillian Wald, you have never been stopped by the impossible. Think of when you first plunged into this noisy, bustling neighborhood."

Bumped and shoved by pushcart vendors hawking overripe fruits and vegetables . . . acrid fish . . . the stench was suffocating. Flies and uncollected buckets of sewage everywhere. I must have been the most naive person south of Houston Street. Imagine a million and a half human beings crammed into overflowing dilapidated tenements all in a twenty-block radius the size of a small Kansas farm. I remember thinking, if only the people in power knew what it is like here, they would do something about it.

Twenty-three years since my baptism by fire.

I saw a small timid face peer around the classroom door in the midst of my lesson on home nursing. I beckoned the frightened girl in and she tugged on my skirt. "My mother. My mother. Baby. Blood. Come, please. My mother, here. You come. Please." She tugged on my skirt.

I gathered up the sheets of the bedmaking lesson in my hand and she led me through the steady rain, past piles of garbage. Up manured, muddied streets. Asphalt, asphalt, why no asphalt? Its use was well established uptown. Down Hester and Division we went, to the end of Ludlow. Across a foul courtyard with reeking open privies, we groped our way up a pitch-dark rickety stairway. The sudden shock of a tiny hand on the railing. The fear of trampling a child, always hoping for a sound to warn me where to tread. How long we fought for landlords to light hallways.

I opened the door. A mother and baby lay on a vermin-infested bed, a bed encrusted with dried blood that had been soaked by two days of hemorrhaging. She lay there, too weak to move. A victim of the cruelest, most contemptuous neglect. Abandoned because she could not pay the full doctor's fee.

I recognized the woman. She was enrolled in my course, hoping to qualify for nurse's training. It was the depression of '93. There was no work. No access to the most rudimentary sources of sanitation. Her husband, crippled, had taken to begging on street corners. He spoke no English and had been unable to enlist help when his wife began hemorrhaging.

They were a family of seven living in two cramped dismal rooms. Wooden boards covered the floors and lined the walls like pantry shelves. They rented these spaces out to other immigrants for a few pennies a night. Such is the origin of our charming word, *boarders*.

Impossible.

I rolled up my sleeves and sent the older children down to the courtyard pump to relay buckets of water. I washed and clothed the baby. I bathed the woman (her bleeding had stopped), scrubbed the floor, made the bed using the fresh linens I had brought. I sent the father out with money to buy food and assured them, "I will return." Their gratitude was overwhelming. I could hardly free myself from their embraces.

For half an hour I roamed, dazed, through the streets, haunted by this impoverished, uprooted family. The sweetness of love in their home.

I walked. I walked and walked. Suddenly I felt a touch on my forehead. Here was how a nurse could be useful, independent of the medical establishment. I was earning my M.D. So was

Mary Brewster at the Women's Medical College. Why? Not because nursing duty required twelve-hour days, caring for patients, polishing brasses, cleaning wards, and washing dishes. No, we wanted our own M.D.'s because of how badly the doctors treated the nurses. As their handmaidens. I am not anyone's handmaiden. One doctor even had the nerve to chide, "Nurse Wald, you have encouraged this patient to laugh before I ordered you to do so." He was serious.

But now I rejoiced. No more medical school. Right here, the voices in this teeming neighborhood desperately cried out for our direct and immediate nursing skills. I could not defend myself as part of a society that looks the other way, that permits such conditions to dominate.

I called on the sponsor of the home nursing course, Mrs. Betty Loeb, at her 38th Street brownstone. Her son-in-law, Mr. Jacob Schiff, was present. I said, I have seen children scarred by rat bites. A small boy, sitting on a low stool stitching knee pants, his face flushed with chicken pox. A girl in advanced stages of TB, moistening cigarette papers with her lips. In the streets, little coffins for sale, stacked up mountain-high. I have seen a man standing on the street next to his family's possessions, thrown out. Evicted. It is Friday night. A woman lights the *shabbos* candles, and boils water in covered pots. Too proud to let her neighbors know there is nothing to eat for the Sabbath. The pride—the struggle for dignity—the mean deceit played on these new arrivals to America with their visions of open farmland, green fields, gainful employment.

Jacob Schiff and Betty Loeb agreed to pay Lillian Wald and Mary Brewster one hundred and twenty dollars a month to cover nursing supplies and living expenses in a fifth floor walkup. Our only requirement, "the convenience of a bathroom. Rumor has it there are only two south of Houston Street." Mr. Schiff arranged for official badges from the Board of Health. To detach ourselves from the stigma of charity and the missionaries, we charged ten to twenty-five cents for a home visit. Those who could not afford to pay were able to accept our services as a neighborly act.

At first the neighborhood boys did mistake us for missionaries. We were bombarded with vegetables. Actually, rotting cabbage and tomatoes. But soon we had the culprits organized into the Nurse's Settlement soccer club. "Miss Wald, Teacher, the other teams tease and taunt us with 'Noices! Noices!' Please, please, please change the name from Noices!" Little Ernie Brofsky's humiliation was too much for me. From then on we were known as the Henry Street Settlement House.

Mr. Schiff became my friend of friends, and taught me how to raise money. "Style your requests for money to fit the moods and persuasions of potential supporters. Remember their birthdays and anniversaries." He bought us this beautiful Georgian house—265 Henry Street. Built in an earlier time when lower Manhattan was fashionable. Our reputation spread quickly. "Go see the two young ladies who will listen!"

Years later I learned Mrs. Loeb told her daughter, Nina, "I have had a wonderful experience talking with a young woman who is either crazy or a genius."

Now we have seven houses; plus one on Seventy-ninth Street for the Visiting Nurse Service; plus one on Sixtieth Street staffed by Negro nurses; seven summer camps in the country; three storefronts for milk stations and clinics; ninety-two nurses who make over 200,000 home visits a year; three thousand club members; countless students in our classes. And the Neighborhood Playhouse. The most exciting, innovative theater in the city, bringing culture and beauty to the long-denied.

Yes, Mr. Schiff, your predictions were right. I now spend half my time raising money. You know I want Henry Street to serve as a model for what the federal government could do for its citizens. But the campfires of war burn in President Wilson's eyes. Peace and negotiation have come to be unpatriotic. Mr. Schiff, dear friend, you have supported me from the very beginning. Even when we disagree about trade unions. Will you continue to support me if I go to Washington today?

5:35 A.M. The train won't wait.

Mr. Schiff, this is a moment in history that may not come again for a long, long time. You approved when the AUAM helped to avert a war with Mexico. We can do the same with Europe. We can try. I will remind the president how the AUAM set up peace talks between the U.S. and Mexico—taking place in El Paso this very minute. In spite of the militarists jumping up and down for us to invade Mexico. In spite of paying Nicaragua three million dollars for a naval base from which to attack Mexico. In spite of General Pershing and his troops crossing Mexico's border on the pretext of chasing bandits. Using two Negro cavalry regiments to draw fire—the NAACP made that fact public.

How can we make the people in Washington care that war and hatred and prejudice go hand in hand?

Just a few short years ago Henry Street's Community Hall was the only location in the entire city where colored people and white people could sit down and meet together. I suggested a dinner party at the house following the meeting. But the formal, meticulous Dr. Du Bois said, "Impossible, Miss Wald. A meeting is one thing. But if reporters found out the two races sat down to a social dinner, they would attack us all for promoting miscegenation. The new NAACP would be ignored." "Dr. Du Bois, two hundred members of the conference cannot sit down—our house is too small. Everyone will have to stand for a buffet supper." That party was a great success. The NAACP was well launched. Dr. Du Bois was very pleased.

I once made a house call to a Negro youngster, Bill Lattimore. His little friend pointed to me and whispered, "Bill, is she your grandma?" I swept that little boy up with such a hug. His innocent eyes saw only my years, not my "white" skin.

At what age does the vision harden for children—hardened, so hardened Congress can't even get an antilynch law passed.

5:50. Why am I not ready by now? I'm terrified to go. Terrified not to go. I have never missed a train. Will this be another Lillian D. Wald first? "No, no," I said to the delegation. "Don't bother to pick me up. I'll take the streetcar. It will be quicker. I enjoy public transportation. I fought for it and I'll use it."

Kitt wanted to give the house a brand-new shiny automobile. The idea. No, indeed. Not that kind of extravagance as long as I can hop on and off a streetcar.

(SHE *takes out a packet of letters tied with a ribbon.*)

Oh, Mabel Hyde Kittredge, how I long to bare my soul to you—my doubts.

I know what you would say.

"Lil, you fool everyone else into forgetting you're mortal. Don't fool yourself. All you can do is make your best case to Wilson. Courage is as infectious as fear."

But do I have the right to jeopardize the settlement?

(Begins to read from a series of Kitt's letters.)

"Just because you despair over the war—just because you momentarily lose your confidence—I never think you are weak because you dare to be human."

"I would very much like to meet you on a desert island or a farm where the people cease from coming and the weary are at rest—will the day ever come?"

"Come on out to Monmouth. The big restless, restful ocean is rolling to my door. Even you must want the ocean at times instead of Henry Street."

Kitt, if only you hadn't tried to ease me away from my work here—

(Reads.)

"For your health, Lil. For your own good. I'm so tired of an endless lot of people forever coming to your door, presenting you with unsigned papers and a multitude of requests. It makes me lack that perfect sympathy with 'work for others' as exemplified by the settlement."

Oh, Kitt, Kitt, don't you see the reason "Jane Addams and Mary Rozet Smith have shared their lives for over twenty years" is because they share a vision? They bring out the best in each other. That's my definition of love. Someone who brings out the best in you. Henry Street brings out the best in me.

One night two men from the Board of Education dropped some of us off here after the meeting proposing free school lunches. Before they pulled away from the curb we overheard their conversation: "Those women are really lonely." "Why under the sun are they lonely?" "Any woman without a man is lonely."

We're a family here at Henry Street. None of us feels lonely. I am not lonely. In all the world there isn't any group with more sparkle, more ability to abandon themselves to genuine good times than the people who are not self-absorbed in their own small cosmos. I have never been lonely.

Oh, how Mama wanted me married. The rounds of teas and cotillions in Rochester. At Miss Cruttenden's English and French Boarding School for Young Ladies and Little Girls, the youngsters would stay up late waiting for us to arrive home. They would press our dance cards to their eager hearts, and entreat us to tell them all about our suitors. My light-blue satin swirled with the waltz—the stunning ivory velvet evening cape—the silver crocheted party bag—my hair swept high atop my head—On my arrival the young men dashed up to me. My dance card was always filled. I love to dance! I love to dance!

When my younger sister, Julia, married Charles P. Barry, the son of a wealthy Irish family in Rochester, Mama and Papa beseeched their restless Lillian to accept any one of a number of proposals for marriage. But I didn't want to be married. I had been challenged at Miss Cruttenden's—Shakespeare, logarithims, astronomy, Darwin . . .

When I was eighteen, studying at Miss Cruttenden's, Emma Goldman at sixteen had just joyfully arrived from Russia to live with her sister. Life in Russia is impossible for Jews. The Czar orders them to live in an impoverished area known as the Pale. Whenever there are outbreaks of resistance, savage pogroms follow. Everybody dreams of America.

Emma Goldman expected America to be the land of opportunity. Instead she sewed buttons on heavy overcoats, ten-and-a-half hours a day, six days a week, for two dollars and fifty cents. The American Beauty roses on her boss's desk cost more than her monthly salary. Miss Goldman wasted no time at all learning about trade unions and how to call for strikes.

It is inconceivable to me now that I knew nothing of Emma Goldman's organizing activity at Garson's Clothing Factory, right next door to my own uncle's textile factory.

The first time I ever understood strikes came with a knock on the door here one evening. A young neighbor asked for my help in organizing her cigar-making shop. "Miss Wald, is it ladylike to form a union? Will any man want to marry me if I do?" Union? Shop? The next morning I ran to the local library as soon as it opened to find out what she was talking about.

Emma Goldman is a true fighter and I admire her for that, even though after a visit here she scoffed, "All you do is teach boys and girls how to eat sponge cake with a fork."

I have heard that J. Horace Harding is wavering in favor of the war. But the McCormicks, the Warburgs, and the Cranes are still with me. The Morgenthaus. The Belmonts.

I can't believe Leonard Lewisohn would walk out on me. He is a true friend to Henry Street. What a blessed day when he brought his grown daughters down after their mama died. "Dear Lady, my girls are so grieved, please may they work with you for a while? Teach piano or voice, a dance class or two?" Alice and Irene. At first, such endearing shy girls. *Alirene* I call them. When they began here, their friends treated them as scandalous rebels. "Isn't it just too appalling for words down there?" Soon Alirene were swept up by the excitement. "Leading Lady, we are renouncing marriage to dedicate our lives to the welfare of the East Side immigrants and to our greatest love, the theater."

Who would have thought their magnificent street festivals with casts of thousands would lead to our beautiful Neighborhood Playhouse on Grand Street.

Lily Lubell, the now famous Lily Lubell, was originally our big darling at the Playhouse. She was brought to us by her older brother to perform in the first street festival in 1912. Lily instantly captured my heart. Her first role, high up on a ladder, was a daisy in the "Three Impressions of Spring." She played a daffodil after that.

Everything we do at the Playhouse creates controversy. We lost two conventionally minded sponsors with our first production based on the Old Testament story of Jepthah's daughter. "The dancer's feet were bare! Bare!" I explained, "Irene Lewisohn studied with the great Kongo Son when we were in Tokyo. Do you know how rare an honor it was, breaking a taboo of tradition that the Noh Theater is for men only?" "Miss Wald, this is civilized America and bare feet are lewd!" *Lewd*, he said. Irene's measured, balanced steps following the old Japanese master lives as a moment of eternal beauty in my mind.

More controversy. Recently a cartoon in the Yiddish press showed "Miss Neighborhood Playhouse" slamming the door in the face of the Yiddish theater. We occasionally do perform Yiddish plays even though our current production is the controversial George Bernard Shaw's *Great Catherine*, starring Cathleen Nesbitt. After all, we have not criticized the Yiddish theater for their current *Doll's House*. They added a fourth act with Nora happily returning to live with her husband.

Our audiences come from all over the city, especially our own neighborhood. The stylish uptown crowd makes our theater a stop on their evening excursions. The number of Rolls Royces and Brewsters outside the theater on a Saturday night!

Uptowners can only be assured of tickets if they are sponsors. Maude Adams, Ethel Barrymore, Ellen Terry, Jacob Ben-Ami, our own dear Lily Lubell, and Blanche Talmud, Paula Trueman, and the Indian poet Tagore with his long white flowing beard. One child asked if he was God. I said, "No, but they're good friends." Actors seek something here the white lights of Broadway cannot offer them. A depth of feeling perhaps—an appreciation.

Whenever I enter the Playhouse, I think of my dear brother Alfred. Alfred loved the theater.

Alfred. I am forty-nine. You were twenty-five when you drowned. I was eighteen. You would be fifty-six. Alfred, was one life. One single life. One precious life lost. One.

And at this very moment, old generals are ordering young men to commit mass murder. Legally. With Russian, French, and English lads on one side of the firing line—and German, Austrian, and Turkish boys on the other. They are given the right to hate. Hatred fairly paralyzes me.

Sides. Sides. Taking sides. And the sides are always changing. Whose side are you on? Mr. Schiff has refused a loan to Britain and France because it would be shared equally with Russia. In 1909 he personally went down to Teddy Roosevelt to demand that our government protest the massacre of Jews in Odessa. Mr. Schiff will not aid Russia. But now he is being vilified in the papers here and all over Europe for being pro-German. Even though the U.S. has not taken sides! Wilson insists we are still neutral! Nevertheless Mr. Schiff's entire law firm has been censored and smeared by the press. He even submitted his resignation because his colleagues feel differently about the loan. Of course, out of respect they refused his offer to step down. It's madness.

Mr. Schiff is very strong in his convictions.

I was once and only once the recipient of the famous Schiff temper . . . conviction. He filled up my doorframe with his tall presence, eyes icy blue, shaking a holly wreath from off the front door. "Dear Lady, nativity scenes, St. Nicholas, and a holy night angel atop your Christmas tree are tempting Jewish children away from their faith at an impressionable age! You are a Jewish woman!"

"I am also a member of the Ethical Culture Society!" I felt

as if I had been struck! Pointing to the menorahs in the windows, I countered, "Mr. Schiff, this is a nonsectarian house. I am not leading Jewish children away from their faith. Like you, I believe in assimilation in language and dress. Religion is a personal matter."

I immediately had the Christmas decorations removed. "Lillian, Lillian, stop! I only object to them at Jewish children's gatherings." "That is not feasible," I countered. "You know as well as I do that we are an integrated house."

It was years before I recovered from the anger—the insult. Years before there was another Christmas tree here at the house. Unmerited censure wounds me deeply.

(Begins to write.)

Dear Mr. Schiff,

I am so sorry, my friend of friends, that the papers continue their vicious attack over your denied loan to Britain and France because it includes Russia. I know you are trying to protect me from the same kind of vilification so that Henry Street won't suffer as you have. You are one of this country's most generous philanthropists and patriots. I, with you, encourage a Russian revolution that will end persecution of the Jews and the tyranny of the Cossacks forever. We are all hopeful that Russia can fulfill this dream of freedom and justice—of one nation to be truly run by and in service of its hard-working people. What a beacon of hope that would become on this earth."

Last night at Narcissa Vanderlip's dinner party, your unswerving ideals emboldened me throughout the evening.

A group of Wall Street and business magnates cornered me at cocktails. The men always rush to engage me in controversial debate. "Miss Wald, we want you on the prowar bandwagon. You are losing your reputation for wisely considered, constructive, sane thinking." They were that blunt, even though it was a party.

Then we sat down to dinner and the gentleman on my left launched in, convinced of the error of my ways. "Miss Wald, conscription would be good because the working men do not know how to obey in this country. Discipline would teach them their place and the necessity of doing what they are told." I took a sip of my wine, my Moselle, and calmed myself by focusing on his walrus moustache. I then said, "To be docile and obey when you are underpaid for someone else's profit would indicate a disturbing level of stupidity." Forks stopped in mid-air. "Fortunately our unique system of education teaches people to think and act for themselves. We have to make war obsolete." Conversation stopped in mid-sentence. "Miss Wald," he forced a merry chortle, "war will always be with us." Our hostess coughed, warning me off, but it had gone too far. "I disagree. That is what they said about slavery and it took courageous women and men, Negroes and a thimbleful of our own race, to risk their lives to end the evil practice."

The room stopped breathing. Narcissa quickly introduced the subject of Enrico Caruso's *Rigoletto*.

Mr. Schiff, at least part of my well-earned reputation is still in place after last night. "It costs five thousand dollars to sit next to 'That Damned Nurse Troublemaker' at dinner." Well, in the time between the aspic-truffled pâté and the poached pears chantilly, the gentleman on my left and the lady on my right accepted the privilege of helping those served by the Visiting Nurses. They agreed, "A poor patient has as much right as a wealthy patient to call a nurse." But the comfortable people are getting jittery. Turning away from all but the Nurse Service.

Jane Addams is now called the most dangerous woman in America. She is even labeled a traitor for reporting the facts from Europe's front. Young wounded lads, lying helpless in pain, having to wait too long for the field ambulance, call out constantly for their mothers, beseech their mothers for help. Delirious soldiers again and again possessed by the same demonic memory—the act of pulling their bayonets out of the bodies of the men they have killed. One soldier grasped her hand. "Tell them a bayonet charge does not show courage, but madness. We are fed stimulants and charge forward like insane men. Please, can't the women stop this war?" Jane Addams receives threats on her life for reporting these facts. Except from soldiers who have been in bayonet charges—they thank her again and again in endless letters.

Little Ernie Brofsky is draft age. I don't want to see a bayonet grasped in his hand or breaking through his ribs. The first time he spent two weeks in one of our fresh-air camps, he came running up the hill from his bunkhouse. I was reading *The*

Bluebird to Edith Segal, who loves being read to. She said on her return to the city after her first trip, "Miss Wald, for weeks the buildings swayed like trees." Ernie flew into my lap. "Teacher. I must have swallowed a tadpole in the lake this afternoon. It's alive inside of me here." Together we discovered the lupp-dup, lupp-dup, lupp-dup alive inside of him here. Living with the perpetual noise on Grand Street, he never had the chance to hear the beat-beat-beat of his heart.

The stakes have never been higher. In spite of the risk to Henry Street, I'll find sponsors if I have to go door to door.

(SHE *finishes her letter to Mr. Schiff.*)

Mr. Schiff, like you, I will not turn away from my conscience. I must do everything in my power for peace and justice, and hope that Henry Street will survive and thrive proudly and all the better for it.

Lovingly, Appreciatively, Devotedly, Steadfastly,

Lillian D. Wald.

One hundred thousand French boys died in the first month on the fields of Flanders. President Wilson, no other animal exposes its young to danger. Every species on earth protects its young with its own life. So can we.

CURTAIN

II. *Letters and Speeches of Lillian D. Wald*

Letters

Lillian Wald to Jacob Schiff
1893

This letter details Wald's home nurse visits on July 25, 1893, and reflects the personal, compassionate, take-charge approach that fired her newly chosen work. At first Schiff required daily accountings for each penny spent, then weekly, then monthly. By 1900 Schiff's confidence in Wald's achievements was so firmly established that an annual accounting sufficed. On January 5, 1909, Schiff wrote to Wald, "Indeed there is no necessity for sending me on New Year an account of your activities. . . . You and the ladies associated with you are constant living accounts of your great value. . . ."

July 25, 1893

Dear Mr. Schiff,

My first call was on the Goldberg baby whose pulse and improved condition had been maintained after our last night's care. After taking the temperature, washing and dressing the child, I called on the doctor who had been summoned before, told him of the family's tribulations and he offered not to charge them for the visit. Then I took Hattie Isaacs, the consumptive, a big bunch of flowers and while she slept I cleaned out the window of medicine bottles. Then I bathed her, and the poor girl had been so long without this attention that it took me nearly two hours to get her skin clean. She was carried to a couch and I made the bed, cooked a light breakfast of eggs and milk which I had brought with me, fed her, and assisted the mother to straighten up and then left. In this case the mother has more than the tenement intelligence, the girl is American-

43

born and the family would have been willing to attend the invalid, but she is so ill and emaciated that it required some skill to give her a bath in bed without causing suffering. . . .

Next, inspecting some houses on Hester Street, I found water closets which needed chloride of lime. At 19 Hester, people complained of the closets in the next house, but I found them clean and with sufficient water for flushing. In one room, I found a child with running ears, which I syringed, showing the mother how to do it, and directed her to Dr. Koplick of the Essex Street Dispensary for further attention. In another room there was a child with "summer complaint" to whom I gave bismuth and tickets for a sea-side excursion.

After luncheon I saw the O'Briens and took the little one, with whooping cough, to play in the back of our yard. On the next floor, the Costria baby had a sore mouth for which I gave the mother borax and honey and little cloths to keep it clean. This baby we had sent last week to the dispensary for eczema. My next call was to Mrs. Gittleman, 31 Norfolk Street, fourth floor, to whom a lady had directed me. I accomplished nothing there, for the woman, though not robust, had recovered from her illness and was doing her washing. Though supporting her old mother, five children and herself by peddling, she was doing it decently, and the children and the place looked clean and cared for. The eldest boy of 12 provided the rent, working in a shirt factory. The next day I made it possible for the whole family to go to the Hebrew Sanitarium Excursion. As she had taken two days from her business for the washing and house-cleaning and could not afford another, I gave her sixty cents the same night. This is the sum she might have earned that day and forty cents for street car fares to the ferry. This of course was not absolute necessity, but the mother has been having some pulmonary trouble and the washing she had done was the accumulation of hers and the family's during and since her illness, and a day in the country to that whole family did not seem expensive at one dollar, even if I took the money from the emergency fund. . . ."

I am,
yours faithfully,
Lillian D. Wald

Lillian Wald to Sylvia Pankhurst
1912

Wald's June 14, 1912, correspondence to leading British suffragette Sylvia Pankhurst concerned letters of support from prominent U.S. citizens Oswald Garrison Villard, publisher of the New York Post, then a liberal newspaper, and the progressive magazine The Nation; and Dr. Henry Moskowitz, a social work colleague of Wald's who resided at Henry Street in the 1920s when men were admitted as residents. Wald refers to Alice and Irene Lewisohn, who were in close touch with the Pankhursts and the British women's militant campaign for votes. Emmeline Pankhurst, Sylvia's mother, led a window-smashing protest in London's West End on March 1, 1912, and was arrested, tried, and sentenced to nine months' imprisonment. She was released on June 24 and re-arrested many times thereafter. The British women referred to themselves as suffragettes whereas those in the U.S. movement preferred suffragists. While this letter documents Wald's personal support of the international suffrage movement, it also shows how she generously used her access to influential people, denied to her more militant sisters, in support of that movement.

Miss Sylvia Pankhurst
4 Clement's Inn, Strand
London, England

June 14, 1912

Dear Sylvia,

I hope the letters you wanted for "Votes for Women" arrived in good time. Mr. Villard and Dr. Moskowitz wrote to me that they would send them immediately, and one sent me a copy of his letter, so that I am sure that unless the mail miscarried, you had evidence of sympathy. I am sorry to say that I could not get everybody to write the letters for various reasons, all of which I hope to have time some day to write to you.

I am sending this belated note to you with many apologies. It has been literally impossible for me to get through my daily mail. I know that Alice and Irene have kept you informed from time to time of our movements here and are concerned about the affairs in England, particularly those affecting your family. They have permitted me to read your interesting letters, and we all wanted to keep posted on the situation.

Naturally, I am deeply grieved that your mother must submit to the imprisonment. If you communicate with her, please give her my deep love, and tell her how much we care this side of the Atlantic.

I am about to start for Cleveland, Ohio, to attend the several national conferences there and from there to Chicago to attend the Presidential Convention. Mr. Roosevelt has announced his intention to include an equal suffrage plank in his platform. Probably the other candidates will do the same. The newspapers will doubtless publish the facts of this before my letter reaches you.

I hope you are taking care of yourself,—at least as much as you can, and that your mother is not suffering physically.

Affectionately yours,
[Lillian D. Wald]

Jacob Schiff to Lillian Wald
1914

This letter, written the day after an intense argument between Schiff and Wald about her having placed a Christmas tree in the Curtis Kindergarten, which she ran at the settlement, reveals the dynamics their disagreements could take on. Schiff is unable to enjoy an intimate music salon at Eda Kuhn Loeb's and retreats upstairs to set Wald straight. Wald, deeply wounded by what she considered unjust criticism, banned Christmas trees from Henry Street for years. This incident provided me with a rare insight into her need to retaliate when misunderstood, or when she experienced a loss of control.

Dear Miss Wald,

While they listen to music on the lower floor, I have found my way to Eda Loeb's writing desk to free my mind after the discussion we had last evening and which I clearly saw, annoyed you. This I regretted, but nevertheless I feel I could not have done differently, than to be frank with you. As I have been,—after you told me as frankly that the Curtis Kindergarten was *absolutely* frequented by Jewish children. I have the greatest respect for every religion, for traditions, customs, and even prejudices in whatever religion these may be found, and if there were a preponderance of Christian children in the Curtis or any other Kindergarten they ought to have a Christmas tree and a proper celebration, notwithstanding any minority of Jewish children, who then could stay away or attend just as their parents might wish. But it is both unpardonable and unjustifiable to tempt little children into the customs of a religion foreign to theirs, innocent as this may appear to be, and this must not be tolerated. If as you have said to me you have banished the Christmas tree from 265 Henry Street in deference to my desires, you must have misunderstood this entirely, for nothing is further from me, than the wish to deprive your gentile co-workers from the pleasures of a festival which is peculiarly their own, and as far as I am concerned I would beg you not to suppress in the future any Christmas celebration at 265 Henry Street, so long as such is intended for those who have the right to it.

You know, I want you to understand me in everything, and I hope you can follow the frame of my mind in what I have said to you.

With cordial assurances, I am, always,

Sincerely yours,
Jacob M. Schiff

Lillian Wald to Jacob Schiff
1915

Wald was repulsed by the film Birth of a Nation, *and she hoped to enlist Schiff's prestige and wide-reaching influence to condemn the film's danger-ous white-racist imagery and distorted celebration of Ku Klux Klan history. This letter is instrumental in understanding Wald's position on race rela-tions.*

Henry Street Settlement
New York

Main House
265 Henry Street

March 9, 1915

Mr. Jacob H. Schiff
52 William Street
New York

Dear Mr. Schiff:

I believe that someone has approached you concerning the film of the Clansman now being presented at the Liberty The-atre under the name of "The Birth of a Nation." There has been very great objection to the film because of the two scenes depicting the attack of a colored man on a white girl, ending in his lynching, and the attempt of a mulatto leader of the blacks who had been educated by a white northern man to force the latter's daughter to marry him. It seems that Mr. [Oswald Garrison] Villard and the people who befriend the colored race have exhausted every legal expedient. Several lawyers, among them Mr. Swain of the firm of Paul D. Cravath, have shown their interest. And several Southern people have expressed themselves strongly in condemnation of the film. The Board of Censors refused to sanction it even after the film company made some modifications—modifications, however, which do not sat-isfy the reasonable objections.

In a recent issue, in the "Moving Picture World," a review of the film says the following in part: "The tendency of the second part is to inflame race hatred. The negroes are shown as horrible brutes, given over to beastly excesses, defiant and criminal in their attitude towards the whites, and lusting for white women. Some of the scenes are plainly morbid and repulsive. The film, having aroused the disgust and hatred of the white against the black to the highest pitch, suggests as a remedy of the racial question the transportation of the negroes to Liberia, which Mr. Griffith assures was Lincoln's idea."

I am writing to you because it seems to some people that you could present to some of those who are interested in the film your own personal abhorrence of anything that is likely to arouse race hatred and prejudice. I do not know Mr. Felix Kahn, but I am told that he might use persuasion upon Mr. Griffith and Mr. Aitken, who own the film, and who are also interested in the Mutual Moving Picture Company, in which I am told, Mr. Felix Kahn is very much interested.

When "Uncle Tom's Cabin" was produced recently in moving picture form in the South, the name was changed to "Old Plantation Folks" and objectionable incidents, such as the whipping post, were eliminated. And I am told that in order to meet the objections, Legree was made a "saint." Southern people feared that the play in its original form might arouse sectionalism.

I do not know that you can take this matter up in the few days left before your departure; but if there is no redress in law, though the film may very well incite the colored people to riot,—they feel so strongly about it—there is nothing left but to exert influence upon those who are involved in the production. I do not understand at all that Mr. Kahn has any direct or indirect share in this objectionable production, but it is considered possible that he might be stimulated to persuade the men, Mr. Griffith and Mr. Aitken, who in another way are associated with him in the film business—at least, so I am informed.

Faithfully yours,
Lillian D. Wald

Attached to this letter was a copy of a two-page affidavit Wald signed on April 6, 1915, as part of the movement to stop the distribution of the film:

Miss Addams of Hull House, Chicago, and I saw a performance of the second act of the film drama called "The Birth of a Nation." We were both painfully exercised over the exhibition.

I should say that the authors' interpretation of the period of reconstruction and its presentation at this time is a grave injustice to the colored people and to my mind is fraught with danger to any community that permits it to be given. . . .

Lillian Wald to Jane Addams
1915

Before the United States entered World War I, Jane Addams spent time at the European front and returned filled with stories of atrocities, including the military's abusive coercion of soldiers at the front to take drugs before bayonet attacks. Wald refers to several "knights of the pen" (journalists) who criticized Addams' outspoken outrage against the war machine. Wald had taken Addams' suggestion to initiate a movement to keep the United States out of Europe's war and to harness U.S. power to propose a conference of neutral nations. This letter is one of the first calls that led to the formation of the American Union Against Militarism and demonstrated her unqualified dedication to the priority of peace.

July 14, 1915

Dear Lady,

Richard Harding Davis, Everett Wheeler and other knights of the pen are resenting your statement concerning the doping of soldiers before bayonet charges. I believe you take the *Times*, but if you do not, I will save some of those clippings, in case you should feel inspired to answer.

Mr. [Paul] Kellogg and I are calling together the group of social workers who met here, to take some action on your proposal. It seems to us that if the different sets of people all over the country did the same, it would be valuable.

Mrs. Benedict [Crystal Eastman] has wanted to create a committee to do that, and Paul Kellogg and I, after conferring about it, think it would be desirable to have a representative from each of the various peace and anti-armament leagues, societies, committees, etc. to develop a plan for immediate and widespread publicity to indicate the desire on the part of Americans to have the neutral nations get together.

Love to the dear folks with you,
Yours devotedly,
Lillian D. Wald

Miss Jane Addams
Hull House
Bar Harbor, Maine

Have you anything to contribute to this? Perhaps you could get time to dictate a letter.

Lillian Wald to John Haynes Holmes
1916

The Reverend John Haynes Holmes of Manhattan's Church of the Messiah was a close political ally of Wald's in the AUAM. Her candid description of the dinner party in this letter gave me material with which to illustrate in the play her boldness, spontaneous wit, and keen intellect. I interlaced several strands from my research around the concept of the dinner party: "forks stopped in mid-air"; the responsibility of white people in race relations; and her quip about how much it costs to sit next to her.

February 25, 1916

Dear Dr. Holmes:

Thank you very much indeed for writing so fully to me. I was a little anxious about you myself last Monday, for you looked to me then as if you were having or had had a headache. Of course you ought not to be strained to the breaking point. Doubtless if the campaign [for peace] should get to fever heat you will be able to help out with the occasional speeches.

I agree with you about the necessity of getting arguments presented to audiences, permitting them to think it out in one's presence. I am very glad that you told me about your experience in the Church, for it is a great help in presenting the arguments to know that you can get a reaction from business men.

Last evening a group of Wall Street and business magnates cornered me at a reception to let me know how disappointed they were in me. They intimated that I was risking my reputation for wisely considered, constructive plans, though of course they did not say that quite as bluntly as it was a party; but I knew that they were convinced of my error. Incidentally one of the gentlemen observed that conscription was good because the working men did not know how to obey in this country! His idea was, of course, that this would teach them their place and the necessity of doing what they were told. That, at bottom, is the greatest danger of conscription. In England the working people, I understand, are convinced that it is conscription not so much for this war, but conscription that will be industrial after the war is over.

If you will give us your wisdom as to getting the speakers and arranging the programs, you will be doing a very great service. Miss Eastman is very good, but I feel that since we are so conspicuous and practically stand alone in this anti-militaristic movement, we must be very careful that every stroke tells and that we make no foolish blunders.

I should like above all things to speak to your Forum, but I am a reluctant speaker. I dislike speaking more than any one of the obligations that the Settlement brings to me, and I believe that such value as I have lies in speaking to the small groups that gather around the table or in corners at parties. I keep at it morning, noon and night; my entrance into a room is invariably the signal for the men (more than the women) to group about me and to begin to argue. Moreover, I think that the people in your Forum have heard the arguments so well presented that perhaps it would be a mistake for me to come in. However, I am trying to get something together that will show the extent to which the movement has gone, which we designate as hysteria. If I can get the evidence together in an impressive manner, I will let you know and present that side of it to your people some night.

It has been a very great pleasure to work with you on the [Anti-Preparedness] Committee. I hope very much that you will come some evening and see one of our lively performances at the Playhouse. Unfortunately, as the performers are either working or at school, all performances take place over the weekends. Are you ever free on Saturday evenings? It would be such a pleasure to have you come to the Settlement some time.

With cordial regards, I am
Sincerely yours,
Lillian D. Wald

Dr. John Haynes Holmes
Church of the Messiah
Park Avenue and 34th Street
New York City

J. Horace Harding to Lillian Wald
1917

J. Horace Harding, Chairman of the Board of American Railway Express and a financier, withdrew his support from Henry Street in 1917. This letter is representative of what Wald faced when her philanthropic sponsors disagreed with her politics. Harding's harsh words regarding the AUAM were an attempt to break her brave adherence to her principles.

Max Eastman, Crystal Eastman, and Amos Pinchot (progressive Republican governor of Pennsylvania and a conservationist) all worked with Wald in the AUAM.

J. Horace Harding.
Post Office, Rumson, N.J.

Telephone, 386–Rumson
Telegraph,
Express, Seabright, N.J.

4th August 1917

My dear Miss Wald:
It has been my pleasure to contribute in the past to your work in connection with the Henry Street Settlement, but I

am much concerned about your activities and association with the group described as "Pacifists" or the "American Union Against Militarism."

I read with regret your signature to advertisements published before our declaration of War against Germany, which I felt were greatly against the interests of this Country. I read with deeper regret that you continue the agitation and association with such characters as Max Eastman, Crystal Eastman, Amos Pinchot and others of the same ilk.

Before our declaration of War I thought the attitude of that party was questionable. I now feel their attitude is disloyal and bordering on the line of Treason. They are trying to weaken the arms of our Government instead of lending aid at a time when our Nation's life is at stake.

If you are really in sympathy with such agitators as it appears to be the case from public print, I feel that I am so out of sympathy with your views and associates that I prefer to extend my financial aid to works that you are not connected with and will discontinue my contributions to the Henry Street Settlement.

If I am mistaken regarding your position I will be only too happy to hear from you.

Very truly,
J. Horace Harding

Lavinia Dock to Lillian Wald
1931

Lavinia Dock frequently wrote up notes for Wald to draw on for her speeches and articles. The following is an excerpt from a packet of material she sent for Wald's speech on Armistice Day, November 11, 1931. Entitled "The Theoretical Case Against War Is Complete," it consisted of twelve handwritten pages with newspaper clippings pasted between paragraphs. Dock's observations engendered the last lines of my play.

Moloch is the biblical name of an ancient Phoenician and Ammonite god, to whom children were sacrificed by burning.

. . . One of the most astonishing revelations after world war was that revelation of the mental attitude of parents and other older people. They seemed completely subjected to a performed superstition. A sense of inevitability, of inescapable necessity: in short a fatalism that could no more be combatted than that of the worshippers of Moloch or the fierce [ancient] Gods of Central America. With many unlettered but religious people there was a literal substitution of God for Moloch.

"No (they would say) we think war is terrible but it is sent by God to punish mankind for its wickedness."

This feeling persisted even after the war—such parents would never say, "There must never be another war." This fatalism was shared by (educated) parents.

"What's the use?" they would say—"There will always be wars and I don't want to have my own boys stay at home while others fight."

More shocking and repulsive was the display among socially secure or privileged parents of an actual sentiment of adoration of what they called "heroic" qualities and bearing shown by other parents, or victims, during the tragedy—a veritable mental attitude of worship it was. Though called "sentimental" it was worse or more deep-laid than sentimentality. It was pure idolatry—no other emotion could bring parents to a deliberate consent to thrust their own young into the fiery furnace of war—as they once laid them in the red hot arms of Moloch.

No animal would expose its young to danger. Every beast protects its cubs with its own life. . . .

Sources

The letters are from the following two manuscript collections: Lillian Wald Papers, Rare Books and Manuscripts Division, The New York Public Library, Astor, Lenox, and Tilden Foundations (NYPL); and the Lillian D. Wald Papers, Rare Book and Manuscript Library, Columbia University Libraries:

Lillian Wald to Jacob Schiff, July 25, 1893. NYPL, Box 1, Reel 1.

Lillian Wald to Sylvia Pankhurst, June 14, 1912. NYPL, Box 2, Reel 1.

Jacob Schiff to Lillian Wald, December 2, 1914. Columbia, Box 9.

Lillian Wald to Jacob Schiff, March 9, 1915. Columbia, Box 10.

Lillian Wald to Jane Addams, July 14, 1915. NYPL, Box 2, Reel 1.

Lillian Wald to John Haynes Holmes, February 25, 1916. Columbia, Box 89.

J. Horace Harding to Lillian Wald, August 4, 1917. NYPL, Box 11, Reel 9.

Lavinia Dock to Lillian Wald, notes for a speech on Armistice Day, November 11, 1931. Columbia, Box 88.

Speeches

"Organization Amongst Working Women"
1906

In this speech Lillian Wald hoped to increase understanding and support
for the vital work of the Women's Trade Union League. Founded in 1903,
it sought to educate and politically galvanize women to organize their own
trade unions. The WTUL was a spirited alliance of working women and
middle-class reformers. The League's demands included an eight-hour work
day, equal pay for equal work, and suffrage.

The "large-minded working woman" to whom Wald refers is presum-
ably Leonora O'Reilly, labor leader, reformer, co-founder of the NAACP—
and factory worker from the age of eleven. O'Reilly and Wald had been
allied since they met at the Social Reform Club in 1888.

Wald began her talk with the stunning fact that as early as 1900 over
five million women worked outside the home. Despite all evidence to the
contrary, politicians have continued to cherish the false illusion that wom-
en's place is in the home.

This speech touches on one of the longest-lasting debates within the wom-
en's movement: protectionism versus independence, and later protectionism
versus the equal rights amendment. Here Wald supports protective legislation, or labor laws that would protect women, by limiting the number of
hours per day they could work and the type of jobs they could take, or
shielding them from health hazards in the "dangerous trades" as revealed,
for example, by the White Lead Commission of 1898. But, more urgently,
Wald called for the organization of strong, independent women's trade
unions in order for women to define, to bargain collectively for, and to
achieve their own wants and needs.

Over five million women are at work in the United States according to the 1900 census, over five million removed from the home wholly or in part, over five million who are factors in the industrial world to reckon for themselves, to be reckoned for and to be reckoned with. Despite such figures, as a nation we superstitiously hug the belief that our women are at home and our children at school, and though legislators have at times enacted laws protective to them, regulating hours and in some instances dangerous occupations, as a whole the community—and this includes many of the working women themselves—is reluctant to face the situation frankly and seriously, that women no longer spin and weave and card, no longer make the butter and the cheese, scarcely sew and put up the preserves at home, but accomplish these same industries in the factories, in open competition with men, and except in the relatively few instances of trade organization, in competition with each other.

The introduction of complicated machinery, the substitution of machine-made for hand-made things, and the impracticability of the introduction of these machines into the homes are of course primarily responsible for the transfer of the women workers from the home to the factory and shop. The fact that the women have received their pay in money for their labor under these altered conditions has had probably no little effect upon the changes in their position in the social world, and has helped to give them their distinct place in the industrial consideration. Probably they worked as hard, produced as much under the old methods, but laboring at home for and with the domestic group, they neither had occasion nor opportunity to classify in the larger group of trade and occupation. . . .

There is little reliable data from which to make deductions concerning working women; indeed, we scarcely know more than the numerical facts and are not able to establish reliable theories. From the census we learn that the five millions and more women earning money away from home are increasing in number more rapidly than are the working men, and that the rate of increase is greater than that of our entire female population. These figures are expressive of a possible reversal of the orthodox order of things, potentially involving us in a new order; and they are suggestive, if not explanatory, of the race reduction statistics.

Congress is now considering an application from the Secretary of Commerce and Labor to make appropriation for a thorough Federal investigation of women in industry. This has been earnestly urged by the women in industry themselves through their trade unions, and the Women's Trade Union League, and by others. Because of the dearth of authentic information, and also because of many erroneous and sometimes sensational ideas afloat, it is to be hoped that accurate information of the whole subject will be made possible (through this investigation) and that public opinion not less than educational and legislative plans may be guided by its results. Meanwhile, and because of the paucity of literature concerning the American situation, one must draw upon accumulations of personal experiences and observations for inferences of significance in the movement among the women towards organization. Whether it is an unconscious merging of the interests of the crowd, a movement fraught with signs and portents intelligible and seriously considered by the initiated, what is the attitude of the outsider, what the moral obligation of those indirectly involved? In ten minutes I can hope only to touch upon the attitude of the non-combatants— if the term is permissible—and of those directly involved.

Abroad there have been more protective governmental measures than with us. One English writer says: "Out of the desecration of child life and womanhood recorded in the blue books in the earlier part of the last century came the beginnings of a state control in England of special conditions of health and security for them."

Certain trades have been considered particularly dangerous to women. The recommendations of the White Lead Commission in 1898 practically put a stop to the employment of women in that industry. Many countries have precautionary legislation for women before and after child-birth (see Oliver in "Dangerous Trades"), and all civilized countries forbid their employment in mines.

The International Labor Conference held last year in Berne (every civilized country being represented with the exception of the United States and Japan) made an international agreement to keep women out of manufacturing establishments at night. This is to go into effect in three years from the date of the conference, and covers all manufacturing trades with the exception of a few special industries where the time limit is extended.

Last February (1906) the American Association for Labor Legislation was organized, which in the future may send delegates to this international body. Under date of December 12, 1905, an American Counsul, reporting on this body to the Secretary of State, urged among other things, the advantage to be gained through uniform action by the different nations in regard to prohibition of night work by women in industrial establishments.

In America there is legislation in all States in which mines are situated prohibiting employment of women. In seven States there is legislation which prohibits employment of women to do buffing and glass polishing. Women are also prohibited from working behind bars. There is legislation in many States regarding this, and in those where the laws do not prohibit public opinion serves the same purpose.

There are also the better known restrictions as to hours of work permissible to women—limitation to fifty-eight hours a week in Massachusetts, sixty hours in New York. This law has been judged in the Supreme Court of Illinois as unconstitutional; has been judged constitutional in Massachusetts. Its constitutionality was tested but yesterday in the courts of New York, and it has been enforced for years in Ohio. In this we can see the uncertainty of a uniform enforcement of attempted protection by the States.

I make reference to these statutory measures showing the existence of a public sentiment as to the necessity of guarding the interests of women, and there is yet a seemingly deep-rooted prejudice against regulations by themselves for themselves when expressed in trades unionism, a curious confusion in democratic principles. Law enactment is worshipped and yet law is suspected if made by an absolutely self-governing body, while, to the student, the development of protective legislation for working women seems a preliminary to the establishment of further protection through their own efforts. Law enactment has been and perhaps will be confined to the establishment of a standard for hours and hygienic conditions, leaving the question of wages entirely to the workers themselves.

In the United States, with the fear of special class legislation and paternalism in government, there is, perhaps, greater need than abroad for concerted action for the purpose of guarding and advancing the interests of the workers themselves. What part have the women workers played in this?

Historical precedent, lack of education in administration, and the conventional tradition of women—not any less among those who work—are potent frustrators of strong and permanent organizations. Though some have grasped the elementary fact of the advantage of collective bargaining and are not loth to be advantaged thereby, ignorance among the many of the import of trades unionism must necessarily make progress slow. The hope of marriage, the insufficient trade training, the demand for cheap and unskilled labor in many trades, and therefore the easy substitution in the ranks of the women wage earners are detrimental factors that preclude expectation of a large, general trades union movement among women in the near future.

More definite and therefore perhaps easier to combat, although a very serious obstruction to women's unions, is the sex antagonism, the blind rage against them for taking men's places, and the consequent disparagement and ridiculing by the men of the girls in their attempts to take their place in the industrial world seriously. Men's unions with larger vision, however, and this is more especially true of late, have invited and assisted women, either in separate organizations or with them, and the American Federation of Labor has declared its policy to be "heartily in sympathy and ready to cooperate with any movement to organize women."

The women, despite handicaps, have organized in those trades where special skill is required, and also where the public sentiment among their comrades has been conducive to dignified organizations. For instance, the laundry workers in Chicago for ten years have sent their representative to the American Federation of Labor. The felt hat trimmers have been organized for nineteen years, the cigar makers for fourteen years, and in the boot and shoe work the women are said to be stronger unionists than the men in some localities.

Miss Herron's recent report of "Labor Organizations Among Women" gives us at some length the facts of their history and place in unions, and it is favorable showing on the whole, an encouraging evidence of the working woman's intelligence, and is capable of favorable comparison with the position the "modern woman" has taken in the professions, in civic and educational and social organizations.

The Union Label League, pleading its members to patronage of articles made under union conditions, that is, in union shops, and holding the same philosophy that has gained the respect of the economists for the consumers' league, urges the power of the purchaser to create the condition. Some of the trades unions have auxiliary label leagues composed of the women members of the working man's family.

There has not been a valid economic argument presented by theorist or practical trades unionist that I have not heard from the lips of the leaders among women laborers. They know full well the fundamental economic fact of the essential and permanent inequality between the individual wage earner and the capitalist employer, and that the possibility of an absolutely free contract between them is a delusion. They are well aware that the danger to themselves and to their countless successors lies in the cutting under of prices by the "sweater" and the "poor widow" who has the "freedom" to work all day and all night at home. They speak with eloquence of the devastation of child labor, the destruction to the homes through long hours and "speeding up" in the shops, their deprivation of leisure and therefore the home. "For all we know," said one, "soup grows on trees."

These are the leaders, the forward guard who proclaim their right to engage in industry when they choose to do so, and to enter on terms of justice and with dignity, since the position of women in industry is dignified and should not be parasitic. They are producers, wealth creators and permanent factors, to be dealt with seriously, no better, nor worse than men, but according to their strength, their tasks and ability.

I have refrained from harrowing or romantic tales illustrative of women's struggles, hardships, heroisms, abilities, disabilities, exploitations, temptations, etc., because such illustrations must be familiar to all in this audience, and also because the dignified women I know in the industrial field would, I think, disparage such methods of presenting their cause. For thirteen years, however, I have seen various little groups organize under the inspiration of fine leadership and then melt away. Other groups have replaced them and the experiment has been repeated. Always have I been thrilled by the wisdom and unselfishness of the leaders, and overwhelmed with the pathos of the sacrifice of the standard-bearers and the great odds against them in their struggle.

The more or less ephemeral character of the organizations does not, however, affect the situation materially. Women remain in the trades and will for all time, and it is of grave importance that the best conditions should be established, not for favorable discrimination on account of sex, which cannot be defended, but for just pay for such work as her talents and her ability and her general fitness may entitle her. For this larger end may we not regard them also as students in an educational movement, though perhaps on the whole an unorganized five million still learning the rudiments of the industrial struggle, learning the hard lesson that it may be passed on in their homes with intelligence and comprehension to sons and husbands and daughters. The failure of the single trades union seems to count but little with these students, for never have I known one girl who believed that the principle, insomuch as she had grasped it, was wrong, but always that it was the circumstances beyond her control that prevented continuity of the group, or the misfortunes of strife that broke it up.

The public's attitude towards trades unionism has been prejudiced and the moral vision obscured. Good men and women speak of the menace to individual liberty through regulations and restrictions by unions, while agreeing to, and, in fact, often eager to accomplish this same restriction by legislation. As I have said, it is a great mistake to assume that there is more personal liberty or less in one than in the other. Labor legislation must of necessity act for the young and the immature, but intelligent trades union regulation for women by women has failed to be effective only because of lack of strong trades unions among them. Unless we speed their day they will be working "The Long Day" for small wage and carrying home the unfinished work to sap the strength of the youngest. When women have effective organizations and suitable State legislation, home work, which means sweat work and children's work, will be abolished. Legislation cannot accomplish this alone; the women are in a position to regulate and enforce this if backed by public sentiment.

The saving of the home of the working people rests upon the women. The elimination of the sweated workers is their task ultimately, and their intelligence can be trusted. They know why tuberculosis so often takes their shop-mates, why the shop work so often injures the eyes, why the "speeding up" with new machinery exhausts them, and the best of them believe that the hope of the betterment of women in industry lies in their quickening of industrial evolution, and that with more secure establishment in the trade they will be able to screw up the standard of life and the home bit by bit, and that they are not liable to get this unless they demand it and secure it themselves.

To sum up:

It is significant that, despite discouragement and handicap, the most thoughtful working women persist in their faith in organization, and it must be obvious that several things can be read from their persistency and their success as well as their failures.

1. The educational value for themselves and their families.

2. The evidence of the thought and decision and the parallel in club and social associations of the "new woman."

3. The serious recognition of themselves as permanent factors in the industrial and social world.

4. The belief in the possibility of their industrial organization replacing their present industrial disorganization.

5. Their need of the public's help and sympathy.

It is difficult to close without suggesting some action by the less directly involved public. This struggle of the working woman is not a class matter; it is one for the race welfare, and though there are heroes among them ready "to die for the cause," to establish themselves in better fortunes is beyond their feeble power unassisted by public sentiment. They believe— these most thoughtful working women—that the most direct way to a stable realization of their standards of wages and hours is through their own trade combinations, and that they are helping the employers as well as themselves. They agree to the necessity of that unfortunate law of competition that the conscientious and well-meaning employer is forced to the level of the employer without scruples, because hours and wages regulate the cost of production, and both the conscientious and indifferent enter the market in competition.

The last organization to be formed is the Women's Trade Union League, composed of working women and their allies, men and women who agree to the claim that I have set forth, and who desire to work with the women rather than for them in their efforts to obtain better conditions. The league owes its existence in America to a large-minded working woman, who has many times said much better what I have tried to say for her fellows to-night. She has been for years an organizer of women's trades unions, and holds that to be her highest mission, but she believes now, as do those enrolled in membership in this organization, that it is proper for men and women to give support and assistance to the working women in their efforts for organization, and that they—the public and the working women—need each other to accomplish this. This seems to be a clear call to that part of the community that with any seriousness concerns itself with the welfare and the fate of the women in industry.

"Best Helps to the Immigrant Through the Nurse"
1907

Lillian D. Wald understood the connection between the health of patients and the social, economic, and political realities of their lives. Central to her concept of the public health nurse, also known as the district nurse, was her realization that home visits afforded an opportunity for the nurse to educate the immigrant family on child labor laws, sanitary laws, the danger of exploitation in home industries, sexual hygiene, and the prevention of illness. In a society that "blamed the victim" for all social ills, education and political activity served to allay hopelessness. Wald once said that the word poor was seldom used at Henry Street: "To us it is a weasel word conveying a sense of failure most humiliating to the people who suffer from poverty."

Wald was instrumental, with other nurse leaders and educators, in establishing training for nurses that was based on a holistic understanding of the connection between health and politics, and worked to bring that health care and education to the public. The following, an excerpt from a typed manuscript, is an example of such efforts.

. . . District nursing of today follows the tradition of its earliest conception. It has been used since the beginning of its history to carry propaganda as there has been always an enthusiastic belief in the possibility of the nurse as teacher in religion, cleanliness, temperance, cooking, housekeeping, etc. My argument loses none of its force, I think, if much of this education has seemed to her lost energy because with greater knowledge and wider experience she has learned that the individual is not so often to blame, as she at first supposed. That while the district nurse is laboring with the individual she should also contribute her knowledge towards the study of the large general conditions of which her poor patient may be the victim.

Many of these conditions seem hopelessly bad but many are capable of prevention and cure when the public shall be stimulated to a realization of the wrong to the individual as well as to society in general if [they] are permitted to persist. Therefore her knowledge of the laws that have been enacted to prevent and cure, and her intelligence in recording and reporting the general as well as the individual conditions that make for degradation and social iniquity are but an advance from her readiness to instruct and correct personal and family hygiene to giving attention to home sanitation and then to city sanitation, an advance from the individual to the collective interest. The subject is tremendously important, even exciting, and adds the glamor of a wide patriotic significance to the daily hard work of the nurse. The prevalence of tuberculosis, for instance, brings attention directly to conditions of industry and housing, next to hours of work, to legal restrictions, to indifference to the laws, to possible abuse of the weaker for the benefit of the stronger.

It is splendid vindication of the value of comprehensive education and stimulated social conscience that the district nurses who have had this vision have been the most faithful and hard working and zealous in their actual care of the sick. . . . [The] wider vision [of the district nurse] makes for thoroughness as an all important educational, social and humanitarian necessity where the patients are concerned.

These opportunities ... bear the closest relationship to the immigrants, because they are the most helpless of our population and the most exploited; the least informed and instructed in the very matters that are essential to their happiness. The country needs them and uses them and it is obviously an obligation due them as well as safe guarding of the country itself to give them intelligent conception and education of what is important to their and to our interests. ...

Address to the House Committee Hearing on Establishing a Federal Children's Bureau 1909

Every day at 7:30 A.M., the "family" of residents at Henry Street gathered together for breakfast. Work problems were aired, nursing assignments were made by Lillian Wald, and mail was opened and read aloud.

One morning in 1905 Florence Kelley, a lawyer and head of the National Consumers' League, read aloud a headline announcing that the Secretary of Agriculture was to investigate the protection of the cotton crop from the boll weevil. "Lucky the sick chickens, ailing hogs and oppressed scallops our government takes such a personal interest in," Kelley quipped.

Wald felt a "touch on her forehead," as she put it, something that occurred whenever she was about to make a significant connection. The first child abuse case on record had been handled by the Society for the Prevention of Cruelty to Animals in the mid-1800s. She believed it was time for the federal government officially to provide for the nation's children: "to take the child out of the realm of poetry and pure sentiment into the field of scientific, organized care and protection." For the next seven years Wald, Kelley, and others fought to make the dream of a Federal Children's Bureau a reality.

In April 1912, President William Howard Taft signed the bill that established the Federal Children's Bureau. With social worker Julia Lathrop as Director, the Bureau became one of the most abiding contributions women social reformers made during the Progressive Era. It investigated and documented the conditions of child welfare (including infant and maternal mortality), birth registration, nutrition, juvenile delinquency and the court system, children of single mothers, the mentally disabled, and child labor.

The following is excerpted from the address Wald delivered at the January 1909 hearing on the Federal Children's Bureau Bill, before the House Committee on Expenditures in the Department of the Interior.

. . . Literally the Education Bureau is the only thing that has been established by the government which could be directly construed for the children,—from which it might be said that we as a nation are indifferent.

The Children's Bureau would not merely collect and classify information, but it would be prepared to furnish to every community in the land information that was needed, and diffuse knowledge that had come through experts' study of facts valuable to the child and to the community. . . . As matters now are within the United States, many communities are retarded and hampered by the lack of just such information and knowledge, which, if the Bureau existed, could be readily available. Some communities within the United States have been placed in most advantageous positions as regards their children, because of the accident of the presence of public spirited individuals in their midst who have grasped the meaning of the nation's true relation to the children, and have been responsible for the creation of a public sentiment which makes high demands. But nowhere in the country does the government, as such, provide information concerning vitally necessary measures for the children. Evils that are unknown or underestimated have the best chance for undisturbed existence and extension, and there where light is most needed, there is still darkness. Ours is, for instance, the only great nation which does not know how many children are born and how many die in each year within its borders; still less do we know how many die in infancy of preventable diseases; how many blind children might have seen the light, for one-fourth of the totally blind need not have been so had the science that has proved this been made known in even the remotest sections of the country.

Registration and our statistics on these matters are but partial, and their usefulness is minimized by the unavoidable passage of time before their appearance. There could be no greater aid to the reduction of infant mortality than full and current vital statistics of children, such as no one community can obtain for itself, and for want of which young lives, born to be valuable to society, are wasted. We realize only occasionally, or after the occurrence of some tragedy, how little is known of other important incidents of the children's lives. We can not say how many are in the jails or almshouses, though periodically the country is stirred by some newspaper report such as that of the little boy of twelve sentenced to five years in a federal penitentiary, or that of a little boy confined for some months upon a trivial charge and incarcerated with a murderer, and other evil men and women, in the cell of a county jail. Outside the few states which have juvenile courts, there is chaos in the treatment and punishment of difficult children, and largely because of lack of knowledge concerning this important matter. This information can not be effectively obtained by private agencies. It is too vital to be left to that chance. Only the federal government can cover the whole field and tell us of the children with as much care as it tells of the trees or the fishes or the cotton crop!

I remember that some three years ago, when it was our pleasure to bring this suggestion before the President [Theodore Roosevelt], his first expression of approval was, if I recall rightly, that "It is bully." It was a coincidence that the Secretary of Agriculture was departing that same morning for the South to find out what danger to the community lurked in the appearance of the boll weevil. That brought home, with a very strong emphasis to the appeal, the fact that nothing which could have happened to the children would have called forth such official action on the part of the Government.

What measures for the advantage of the child and the country would the Bureau further? No direct responsibility or administrative function for furthering new measures would fall upon the experts of a Children's Bureau, but proceeding by the experience of other scientific bodies there would be ample justification for employing the best minds of the country for the application of the knowledge gained, by using the stimulus of suggestion and education. It takes no stretch of the imagination to believe that, with the light of knowledge turned by responsible experts upon all phases of the problem of the child, the American people could be trusted, if not with the immediate solution, then with serious consideration, for what appears to be a national apathy is not really so in fact. What innovation in the governmental function would this introduce? This measure for the creation of a Children's Bureau can claim no startling originality. It would introduce no innovation—no new principle—in the function of government. It is along the line of what we have been doing for many years to promote knowledge on other interests, on material matters. Look carefully into the history of the development and present scope of the various bureaus within the authority of the Government, and ample and fascinating analogies will be found.

Other countries, too, have awakened to realize the import of efficient guardianship of their children, have gathered expert information and are using it under the leadership of trained specialists. The French call this development "Child Culture," which implies the use of scientific minds and trained powers, co-ordinated functions, and the protection of the state to the end of efficient manhood through a well guarded childhood. Current literature every day shows the trend of civilized people to fix the responsibility upon the present generation to preserve and cultivate its resources, indeed charging as a crime against us any reckless waste of these. The English children's bill, that within a day or two has become "An Act," is the best example of this as regards the children. That bill is a most remarkable document indeed, covering practically every incident in the child's life that might come within the concern of the Government. Its ninety folio pages constitute a complete code, and reflect not only the wide range of the government's information, but cover every interesting phase of the development of this vital, social and economic matter. A "veritable children's charter," it has been called. The forms of the English government and ours differ. We do not desire the code; details and administration can be left to the states; but we do desire and we most urgently need information, and the best means of broad publicity on all matters relating to the children, that the national intelligence and conscience may be stirred. The full responsibility for the wise guardianship of these children lies upon us. We cherish belief in the children, and hope, through them, for the future. But no longer can a civilized people be satisfied with the casual administration of that trust. Does not the importance of this call for the best statesmanship that our country can produce? I ask you to consider whether this call for the children's interests does not imply the call for our country's interests? Can we afford to take it? Can we afford not to take it? For humanity, for social well-being, for the security of the Republic's future, let us bring the child into the sphere of our national care and solicitude.

Address to a Meeting under the Auspices of the National Association for the Advancement of Colored People at Cooper Union
1914

President Woodrow Wilson took office in January 1913 and during his first term resegregated official Washington, including those federal departments that had previously been integrated. Known as a historian of American government and democracy, he limited his view of democracy to white men and opposed women's suffrage. He also celebrated as "outstanding" history the viciously depraved film Birth of a Nation. *Lynchings and race violence intensified during Wilson's administration. Few white people cared and/or dared to speak out for the lives and rights of black people, and segregation remained a secondary issue in even the most liberal circles. That was the social and political climate Wald confronted in the speech excerpted here.*

Inevitably, as a white person in segregated America, Wald frequently came face to face with her own racism. There is, for example, a painful exchange in her correspondence concerning Senetta Anderson's wish to apply to the Bellevue Hospital Training School for Nurses in 1915. Anderson, a black high school graduate, personally asked Clara D. Noyes, the General Superintendent of the Training School, if she might apply to the program. Noyes discouraged her, and the matter was referred to the NAACP as a discrimination case. Wald defended Noyes' position on grounds that admitting a black woman to the training school would cause the withdrawal of the majority of their students, Southern white women. Moreover, Wald wrote to NAACP attorney Chapin Brinsmead, there were "good training schools for colored women, and their graduates rank well."

Though her vision was limited in the Senetta Anderson case, Wald protested discrimination and in many ways worked to further racial equality. She served on the NAACP Board of Directors as well as on the board of The Sojourner House for Young Girls, *a residence for troubled and homeless black adolescents. Wald was among the first to train and insist on equal professional recognition for black nurses. Henry Street's Stillman Branch,* staffed by black nurses, served a black neighborhood offering classes, clubs, social events, and a backyard playground.

In the following talk, given on January 29, 1914, Wald compares an attempt to segregate a federal department in Washington to the infamous anti-Semitic Dreyfus Affair that had torn France apart politically between 1894 and 1906. Captain Alfred Dreyfus, a Jewish military officer, was falsely accused of treason and imprisoned for years. General Georges Picquart discovered papers that fully exonerated Captain Dreyfus, and risked his own career to make them public.

This question of segregation looms up in my mind as of mountainous significance. I see in it an invidious and subtle poison that is being instilled into our national ideals. It is not because it is a political question, or not so much because it is a personal matter to those involved, though this is of grave importance, and should not be minimized, but it is a moral question that we should not dodge. That question involves an eternal principle, the principle of dignifying the human being which was proclaimed as the cornerstone of our national edifice and reiterated after the experience of eighty-nine years by the best American of them all at the close of the Civil War. Segregation discriminates against the individual without regard to proven worth or ability. No surer way could be found to injure the pride, the dignity and the self-respect of any person or people than to assume that, because of color, race or nationality, they are unfit to mingle with the community.

However helpless the nation collectively may be because of the prejudice and injustice among the individuals who constitute the nation, it commits the country to a standard when it acts collectively. The attempted segregation at Washington, and the immediate widespread effect of it on the country at large, especially the South, is too important for us to dare to let it pass without letting the world know and in no uncertain terms, the judgment of social thinkers upon it.

General Picquart, who died a short time ago, set France right on the Dreyfus matter. In commenting upon his great service to his country, one of his biographers states that General Picquart's conduct in the Dreyfus story is "one of the most striking testimonies that could be cited of the way in which the guarding of a nation's highest interests may depend on the courage, the self-assertion, and the devotion of a few great spirits." It may be called a gross exaggeration to compare the attempted segregation in one of the Government departments to the tragedy of Dreyfus, but it is potentially as grave, and if students of the subject do not make their protest, we may fail to have a Picquart when he is needed. . . .

The nation has taken a great task upon itself when it set out to harmonize the different elements that make up our country, that all may get together for one great purpose, namely, free opportunity to each, that the best type may be developed. There must be confusion in the minds of many who come to us as to the difference between our high national motives and the acts of the individual. I recall that one day, on passing a Chinese laundry, whose industrious workers were known to me, I missed one of the partners, and upon inquiry as to his whereabouts, I was told by the other Chinese that he was in a hospital, because a Christian gentleman had hit him on the head.

I do not want to add to the flame that has been kindled—far from it. Such contribution as I can make to this discussion, such share as I desire to take in this meeting, is to dwell with all the emphasis within my power upon the wrong that we do ourselves when we wrong, or degrade, or injure any of the people who are in our midst. That moral deterioration falls upon people who deliberately wrong others, is equally true of a nation. Prejudice brings in its train fear and hatred, brutalizing forces that are at war with character development. Segregation that is not entirely voluntary as between races breeds these undesirable traits of character. Without claiming the gift of prophecy, one can foresee that our sins, political and social, must recoil upon the heads of our descendants. We commit ourselves to any wrong or degradation or injury when we do not protest against it.

"Suffrage"
1914

Lillian Wald defined herself as "a suffragist, but not an aggressive one." During the fight for women's suffrage, there was a major split in campaign strategies between the two main suffrage societies. The Congressional Union organized parades, pickets, and civil disobedience while the National American Woman Suffrage Association (NAWSA) lobbied legislators and private individuals. Wald chose to remain outside the organizational fray. In this speech, given in February 1914, it is clear she was convinced that the nature and future of social reform depended on votes for women.

Lavinia Dock, Wald's closest friend and most trusted colleague, belonged to the militant branch of the suffragist movement, led by Alice Paul. When Dock wrote to Paul on September 8, 1914, to accept an invitation to serve on the Congressional Union Advisory Council, she explained and defended Wald's personal decision to keep her public distance from the activist suffrage movement:

> *Miss Wald, however, cannot really ally herself exclusively to any suffragist group because she has close friends in all—for instance your invitation to her to join the [Congressional] Union was balanced by women in the National [American Woman Suffrage] Association asking her not to. This is confidential. She decided to remain independent of all and my own judgment for her is that it is best for her to do so. She has first and foremost her own immense responsibilities to carry and she has never lined up with any one group but is friendly with all.*[1]

Years ago, before I had had any experience in community work, like many other young people I believed that politics concerned itself with matters outside the realm and experience of women, and I accepted the conventional dictum that responsibility in political action and knowledge to guide the government were exclusively inherent in men. I very soon learned for myself that public affairs (political and governmental) were concerned with social matters, upon which women had experience and convictions. Later, I realized that many forms of social activity, affecting the welfare of children, the condition of the homes, employment, health matters, hospitals, infant mortality, etc., were to a large extent created, organized and

Letters and Speeches of Lillian D. Wald

administered by women, but that when these matters came under municipal or state control, women ceased to have any authority over them, or indeed had any share in their control, since the vote influenced the choice of the administrators, the methods of administration and the amount of the appropriations for carrying them out. Measures for social welfare, which Society agreed were of paramount importance to the home makers of the nation, ceased altogether to be their affair, politically speaking, and the opinions of women received little or no attention.

An illustration of this: Two or three years ago, when tenement house legislation, which had been enacted through the influence of good people interested in housing reform, was endangered, a request came from those who were interested in the defeat of the bills for an expression of opinion from my neighborhood. I was definitely instructed to have only the *men* send their views. There was not a woman in the Settlement, among the residents or the club members, who did not comprehend the nature of the proposed legislation and the effect it might have upon their homes, and yet it was frankly stated that a petition from women would have no weight in Albany.

I believe that women have something to contribute to the government that men have not, as men have something to contribute that women have not; that their traditions and their experiences combined will make for a more perfect understanding of community needs. This is an expansion of the ideal family control. Women have been told that they can gain their wishes by influence, using their power over some man or men. Dignified women do not wish to be a part of an invisible form of government. They wish to speak directly and openly, and they consider this a more respectful recognition of their influence. They wish to take their share in the responsibility of Society, and to give back what has been given to them.

Many women have worked faithfully for better conditions through philanthropic societies, through social settlements and in other ways, wielding their power in such measure and in such ways as have been open to them. They believe that they can do more, and they also believe that Society will be the gainer when the enormous numbers of women who now have no opportunity at all for expression are given this through the ballot. I remember that during the time of the [Governor] Hughes anti-gambling legislation, a young German woman in our neighborhood said that she wished the women had a vote, for then there would be no doubt of Hughes' election and the will of the women would be heard as to the gambling laws.

In addition to what seems to be the advisability of completing and perfecting the government by making men and women share its responsibility, the inevitability of the extension of the suffrage makes objection seem futile. The whole force of evolution is behind it. Women are going into public life whether they wish to or not. They have gone into factories, into the professions, they are serving on public committees, they are proposing and even framing legislation. The movement is far greater than the demand for the ballot, and seems to be a force irresistible, one that cannot be swept back.

"New Aspects of Old Social Responsibilities"
1915

In this address to Vassar students on October 12, 1915, Wald celebrated women's participation and achievements in the public realm. She heralded an end to the privatization of women as an impetus for an entirely new social order: the "new woman," joined in unity with other women for political power.

Wald always believed it was possible to arouse in each individual the dormant instincts for compassion and justice. She encouraged young women of privilege to appreciate the many opportunities to serve in the public sphere.

This speech illustrates Wald's sense of humor, her deep understanding of the interplay between politics and ethics, and her profound gender consciousness. For a woman to agitate for the rights of women was not only imperative for her happiness, but ethical, ladylike, and womanly. Strong independent women, she reassured her young audience, should be seen by men not as sex antagonists but as complementary partners in the creation of all that was possible between the sexes—an ever-growing "romance of comradeship."

Full of ginger—one of her own favorite expressions—Wald developed her theory that women have a unique gift to contribute to the public domain. She charged women to see themselves as "coordinators of human values," as peacemakers and active nationmakers for national and international harmony.

I come to you with very mixed emotions; pride and pleasure in participating in the celebration of an institution that, from its inception, has carried so many implications of social import; and a very deep regret that, unhappily for us all, the Fiftieth Anniversary of this College is denied the inspiration of Jane Addams' presence, and that a substitute must come in the place of the wise woman of America, the leader, I venture to say, of social thought of her generation. She, too, I am sure, is disappointed not to be here, for during the past month she has spoken several times to me of this engagement.

Sanction for Woman's Position

The business of being a woman has not altered in its essentials since history has been first recorded, and the so-called "new woman" could, if she would, defend her position by time honored custom and the traditional sanction of the ages. The wise book long ago describing the ideal woman of biblical days claimed for her worldly attributes and great efficiency, associated with tender feeling and a social conscience.

"She seeketh wool and flax and worketh willingly with her hands." A consumer and producer.

"She considereth a field and buyeth it; with the fruit of her hand she planteth a vineyard." In the real estate business and an agricultural student.

"She girdeth her loins with strength and strengtheneth her arms." A winner of athletic honors.

"She perceiveth that her merchandise is good; her candle goeth not out by night." An expert and doubtless an advocate of the double shift.

"She stretcheth out her hand to the poor, yea, she reacheth forth her hands to the needy." A member in good standing of the Associated Charities.

"She maketh herself coverings of tapestry; her clothing is silk and purple." A patron of arts and crafts.

"Her husband is known in the gates, when he sitteth among

the elders of the land." The implication here is that she has made a man of her husband.

"She openeth her mouth with wisdom and in her tongue is the law of kindness." Plainly the social worker.

"Give her of the fruits of her hands; and let her own works praise her in the gates." In other words, she is an individual who must stand or fall as she is worthy or otherwise.

Growth of New Social Theory

But the old social theory was established in the belief that the individual was supreme; and then, with civilization's advance, responsibility was extended to cover the family with the tribal group. . . . Now the larger social groups included in the present conception of responsibility bring new aspects of the position that women must take to hold to their importance and their dignity and to be a part of the progress of the evolution of religion, of the sciences, and of the humanities that are the essence of civilization,—not to be the flying buttresses that support the cathedral arches in an auxiliary architectural capacity, but, if inspired and competent, to be even the pillars within the sacred edifice itself. . . . The conception of religion has extended from the individual to society; a true religion fills the need of both. Economics and government and a rational view of religion are based on human needs; and fundamental human needs underlie the so-called labor and women's movements.

Woman and Labor

Years ago when I first became acquainted with the working girls they made the light penetrate to me until I saw that the trade union, even the strike and the boycott, were in reality a part of the struggle of the young women to hold on to their precious inheritances, — shorter hours to enable them to learn to keep the home, to work, to sew, to read, to be courted, and better pay to adorn themselves that they might find favor in the eyes of man. And the theory of individual competition has given place in their minds to the moral conviction of fidelity to socially established standards, for the maintenance of which the individual, even the family, may be sacrificed that the larger group may profit.

Our forebears, working in the home, thought only of the needs of the family. As home work became factory work, the home worker became the factory worker. In the early days she felt little of the social philosophy which was embodied in her service; but that has developed, and with the understanding of collective bargaining broader ethics were established among the working women; and they today consider the individual in industry who seeks her own interests in defiance of group ethics almost an outcast, scorned as "scabs"—as those who have defied the sanctity of family life have been condemned by society; and in this she is mentally and morally the comrade of the modern progressive economists and labor leaders among men.

The new aspect of social responsibility in industry takes organized form among other women who, fitting themselves to the environment of an age of machinery, band together in groups, as in the Consumers' League; the Woman's Trade Union League; and they have not hesitated to use, for sound moral purposes, methods that, not long ago, might have been considered unladylike and unwomanly. Conscientious women of a great city of Illinois joined with church dignitaries to agitate publicly for the boycott of department stores which would not adopt early closing hours; and the Minimum Wage Board of Massachusetts embodies the idea of the boycott by advertising in the counties of the state those employers who fall below the social-industrial standards. Dramatic expression of the new psychology was presented in Connecticut not long ago when a number of women workers conducted a twenty-four hour strike, followed by a Labor Day procession, floats and a steamer excursion, their employer following their demonstration by a public statement of his conviction that the eight hour standard for which they had contested was socially and industrially advantageous. Manufacturers in that town and others throughout the state have followed this leadership. Public opinion supports the wisdom and social value of maintaining this standard, and, where girls are concerned, the emphasis has always been laid on the fact that the conservation of their health and their morals makes them better mothers and better home-makers.

Women in Civics

In Pennsylvania a few days ago, a whole city paid deference to a woman, who, loving trees and beauty in nature, conceived the great thought of transforming an ugly, disfigured city into one of beauty. Through her perseverance and great patience and because she brought knowledge and fact to brace her arguments, she succeeded in getting civic pride and enthusiasm roused to the endurance of an increased tax rate for their seed.

She has carried out into the world beyond her own garden her conviction of the importance of beauty and order and has made the city profit by her powers to secure opportunities for all the children of her city.

In Indiana legislation for better housing has been brought about by a very devoted home-maker. Because she felt that the nation's life rested upon the home and because the home was so precious to her she wrought "beauty out of ashes" for her state and sacrificed the peaceful and quiet enjoyment of her own home until, by force of all the methods and enthusiasms of a zealot, better homes were insured for other families than her own.

The halos that encircled the saints of long ago might occasionally and with propriety be transferred to the pilgrims who, foot-sore and weary, stand at the gates of state capitals petitioning for legislation to ameliorate and reform, fitting themselves to speak a language according to the law and adjusting their powers of persuasion to meet the newer requirements of legislative exigencies.

Women and War

Euripides made the Trojan women's lament sound down two thousand years and but yesterday women gathered across the seas to state the abhorrence of war and on a world stage to declare that they were conveyors of a message for vast numbers of women in every land,—the belief that life is precious and that to destroy it is a wanton and unpardonable crime, a barbarism that women accustomed to band together for the conservation of life would no longer brook. At a stage in history when women were first organizable they came together to protest against war and to offer reasonable substitutes for settling international disagreements.

Women and Nursing

Doubtless the first profession for women (for its roots are set in the care of the young) is that of the nurse; and it has accompanied her progress throughout the ages. It was a woman of the higher education, one who knew her Greek and Latin and whose mind vouched the minds of the erudite of her age, who had a vision of the great responsibility that lay upon her to apply her warm sympathy, her woman's traditional aptitude and trained hands and intellect to the soldiers, the camp, the sanitation of villages in India and at home and, when hideous war was over, to expand her socialized womanly influence to cover the alms houses, the hospitals, to break down the red tape bureaucracy and the antiquated methods of war offices, to write books on nursing and sanitation and protective health measures. This one woman's influence was dynamic, and was so felt around the world. Florence Nightingale lifted the vague, casual, though kindly and devoted, *feeling* of women into organized, efficient and invaluable service; she enlarged the nurse's vision to sympathy for great groups outside her family or particular tribe.

In the last two decades, coincident with a social unrest because of things detrimental to human happiness, the nurse has emerged into public movements. The appeal to her is the appeal of the community. And that is not at the cost of the single patient or the single mother, but because of the sanctity of life and motherhood and the conviction that the mother, as well as the unborn child and the infant newly born, have become the trust of society. These things challenge the attention of the educated nurse today. It has become her responsibility to make practical application in the homes of the people of the results of scientific thought and research. Nurses have united together in a national society that they may help each other, inspire each other that the community may obtain the utmost advantage possible from this age old profession of women. It is now little more than two years since they [first] gathered . . . as an organization [to record] their interest in and identification with the numerous phases of the public health movements and the promotion of right living. There were among them women who had taken the initiative in compelling the public to focus attention on constructive, preventive, supervisory methods, that an active cult of health might be built up. Creative minds among them have been at work that nurses may be directed toward a goal of social betterment; and this marches side by side with the ancient ideal of a consolatory and alleviating service. It is this most modern aspect of nursing that successfully enlists the socially minded woman, because her work has become an essential part of an harmonious whole. The first woman physician in America died only a few years ago and the first woman to study medicine in Holland, is still vigorous and full of zeal for the free exercise of woman's ability, [and] has been in America for the last few weeks, undaunted by war and crusad[ing] for a great human cause.

Professional Women

Women and with them at times far-seeing men, prophetic because they knew the movements of the past, have helped to open up opportunities in the professions, not as special privileges, but to endow woman that her natural gifts might come to full fruition, and not for her, the individual, but for all—womankind and mankind—to serve the community. To adjust her education to meet the new and enlarging need great universities have established chairs of nursing and hygiene and home economics, dignifying old domestic occupations with professional standards.

Women in Politics

I see in those countries and states where political equality has been established demonstrations of self-realization and almost always the development of those inclinations that are traditional. New Zealand, remote and, therefore, not within the zone of local referendum controversy, has—I think not accidentally—the lowest infant mortality rate in the world. In Norway the legislature has lifted a cruel handicap from illegitimate children. Into the realm of Federal control human needs have been brought, as contrasted with material and academic and diplomatic functions of the government. "A Federal Bureau for Children, its chief a woman, one of your own. What new and mannish venture does she embark on? She rouses the nation—or tries to rouse it—to the neglect of the baby. She takes the baby out of the obscure, so often neglected and hidden crib into the full light of publicity. Suffer not this little one to be lost sight of. It is a child of the nation!" This Bureau is a telling illustration of my theme. The former purely sentimental portrayal of the child is replaced by irrefutable mortality data, and these are shown to be related to high rent rates and low wage scales, twin home destroyers. That is one of the things that women do when they function in public life. They exercise their intelligence for the preservation of the things that are important to them and have always been, and always will be.

Task of Women Today

Upon the educated woman evolves the task of re-adapting the social interests of her sex to a changed physical and spiritual environment. She should, as a member in good standing of the great society, be the coordinator of human values. The task of organizing human happiness needs the active cooperation of man and woman: it cannot be relegated to one half of the world. And active cooperation for such noble ends cannot be secured unless men and women really work together. The women have been experiencing the growth of a new consciousness, an integral element in the evolution of self government, and as a result many women believe that *they* can best represent the human interests in government, at least that they can best represent themselves in those measures that immediately concern them and for which tradition and experience have fitted them. They are more earnestly aware of the social responsibility that rests upon them. Colleges and professional schools have prepared the way for the citizenship of women, as have also the factories and the department stores. The restricted, secluded, non-earning woman was logically a dependent and her efforts were confined to the field of her home activity. Time was when the removal of those activities took her abroad and her going constituted a great venture, but we have long since accustomed ourselves to the idea of her transplantation. With the statistics of women who earn their own living before us, no longer can the idea of chivalrous male protection be impressed upon us and nothing really good has been lost. A very fine kind of comradeship—to my mind even a greater romance of comradeship—has been made possible between men and women; and the fear that disturbs some that this altered relationship between men and women may develop a destructive sex antagonism, is, I believe, wholly without foundation.

The roots of public social service and responsibility are deeply planted in the nature of woman and what we are witnessing in our generation are the new manifestations of her unchanged and unchanging interests and devotions.

Her circle of human experience and human feeling has widened. The invisible form of government so long attributed to her has become distasteful because furtive and, therefore, unwomanly. She is capable of doing more, of being more than at any time.

"Give her of the fruits of her hands and let her own works praise her in the gates."

Address to the Women's Peace March Organizing Committee
1914

Women mobilized against the war in Europe from the moment it was declared on August 7, 1914. In this urgent, rousing call for a peace parade, delivered at a meeting on August 12, Wald joined forces with the great antiwar effort which became her highest priority for the next few years.

The parade committee, an ad hoc group of concerned women, urged her to lead the nation's first Woman's Peace March down Fifth Avenue. They thought that her prestige and stature would ensure respectful treatment by politicians and the press.

The parade committee wrote to Wald:

This is the order which everybody here is clamoring . . .
   1st—platoon with mounted police
   2nd—muffled drum corps
   3rd—Miss Lillian D. Wald alone
   4th—Miss Carpenter, carrying peace flag with two ladies from executive staff as aides

*5th—Mrs. Henry Villard in center with two on each side. Then reg-
ular lines of five to follow two feet apart.[2]*

Wald declined and insisted that the position of honor go to veteran peace,
suffrage, and civil rights leader Fannie Garrison Villard. When the march
took place on August 29, 1914, Wald and other members of the organizing
group followed in rank behind Villard. Fifteen hundred women marched,
dressed in black, or in white with black arm bands. Women from the
warring nations of France, Germany, England, and Austria, a contingent
of Black activists, Henry Street nurses in their blue uniforms, religious
groups, socialists, pacifists, trade unionists, all marched silently in mourning
and in unity for a world without war.

This gathering is assembled for a high moral purpose. In the
face of the feeble accomplishment that can only follow, it may
seem a mockery to call the women together to protest; but there
is among many of us an imperative demand for expression at
this time—when the horrifying spectacle of a world engaged in
slaughter fairly unhinges reason.

If you should today vote to take steps for parade or meetings,
you will be giving opportunity for a collective expression of this
protest. Vital and fraternal relationships exist in this city between representatives of those nations who at this moment are
intent upon mutual destruction. In the poorer quarters of the
city this is more in evidence, and women more than men can
strip war of its glamour and its out-of-date heroisms and patrio-
tisms, and see it as a demon of destruction and hideous wrong—
murder devastating home and happiness.

Women are here to reaffirm their protest against war, to
restate their unalterable faith in the righteousness of Peace, the
practicality of mediation—a protest against the outrage upon
the moral convictions of long developed social sentiments, and
to offer their profound sympathy and compassion for the victims
of the European war.

"Women and War"
1915

In spite of Wald's remark to a friend, "I just hate like thunder to speak," this February 1915 address given at the Cooper Union in New York City testifies to her ability to deliver a thunderous condemnation of war. She saw World War I as a grievous regression in a time of mighty industrial expansion. Wald urged women, "unfettered by custom and expediency," to take the vanguard and lead men away from the violent tradition and institution of war.

Just as soldiers in the trenches frequently reached beyond international differences and achieved a simple person-to-person connection, Wald believed that leaders of nations could meet at the conference table and, with the simple gift of speech, resolve their differences.

Her concern was also with language, with how things were named and how words were used and misused. She noted that the cry to battle appealed "to [men's] heroism to be ready to die for their country." To women the cry to battle seemed less heroic, rather an "appeal to go out to kill." Propaganda sanctioned atrocities: to devastate, starve, rape, and murder women and children was acceptable in the name of keeping one's own family secure.

In December 1914 Wald heralded social workers as heroes in a New York Evening Post interview. "Today a vast army of trained men and women are at work in our large cities . . . in its broadest concept their work is teaching the sanctity of human life . . . the social workers of our time are dreaming a great dream, and seeing a great vision of democracy. . . . War is the doom of all that. . . ."

As the staggering body counts came in from the front, and the money for social services began to dry up in deference to the war machine, Dock's words haunted Wald: "What it takes us years to build up, the men in government tear down in a minute."

The People's Institute and the Manhattan Borough section of the Woman's Suffrage Party have called this meeting tonight that women may have an opportunity to emphasize the aspects of war—that terrible scourge of mankind—that react upon them and are most keenly felt by them.

The final abolition of war and the establishment of permanent peace must depend upon the convictions of men *and* women, who are equally responsible as they must be in the final analysis for all measures affecting Society. But never before, during the time of any great conflict, have women been so organized or so self-conscious as now, and it is fitting that the world should ring with their outcry against this blasphemy upon all the things that they hold most sacred.

Time was when the woman buckled on the armor of her lord, and herself held the spear and the lance to defend the home and the child. We had thought that that day long passed, and that Society's efforts were bent to measures that prolonged life, that protected and conserved, but suddenly, without the consent of the people involved, all the structures of civilization, so painstakingly built up, are swept away, and hatred, destruction and contempt for human life take their place. Multitudes of men and women and children in the countries at war are helpless victims, and their judgments concerning wars, and this war, can not be known, at least not until they are recorded in history. We, the fortunate dwellers upon a neutral land, are, through sympathy and actual suffering, involved in their tragedy. Those who suffer call across the waters, and their cry is heard—the cries of little children and those yet unborn.

Women have a message to deliver, and because they are unfettered by custom and expediency, they can point out the hollowness of the appeals by which men have been stirred to battle. Men react to the appeal to their heroism to be ready to die for their country; women would say that the appeal is to go out to kill. Men who love their homes and their children are roused to war fervor "to protect their homes"—but to destroy other homes; "to save their wives and children"—by starving and impoverishing other women and children.

The horrors of war that stir the thinking world have been least noticed by the historians. The violation of women, and even children, is hardly included in the term "atrocity." Yet so abhorrent are these things that the brutality of war passeth understanding, and men and women must so dedicate themselves to this cause that it can never come into the world again.

The voices of free women rise now above the sounds of battle in behalf of those women and children abroad—for it is against women and children that war has ever been really waged. Those women and children are not alien to us. Victims whose stories I dare not tell on this platform are in New York today.

Here in America, on a new continent, with blood drawn

from each of the great nations now in the struggle, we have tried out a great experiment; many races, from many states, have demonstrated the logic and the practicability of mutual relations. Comrades and friends they are. Their children are in school together; their men and women work in the shops and factories side by side. The enmity that is stirred up in order to make men kill each other and to rejoice in the killing, we know to be fictitious.

Stories that demonstrate this are coming across the continents today. I am told of the Jew who bayonetted someone called "his enemy," and as the man fell he called upon the God of Israel in the Hebrew prayer of the dying. The Jew who had done the bayonetting is now insane.

Two English soldiers who lay wounded heard the moans of a man crying out in agony for a drink. Near them lay a German. They crawled to him and tried to lift him. They found his water bottle and put it to his lips. But he said, "Nein, I die—you drink."

Though the hatred and the enmity that have been stirred up are not real, the suffering and the desolation and the outrages that have come to men and to the women and the children are real. These pitiless sacrifices must stop.

In the Neighborhood Playhouse, not far from here, a wonderful performance is being given, based upon the story of the sacrifice of Jephthah's daughter. The recoil from human sacrifice that was sanctioned when done in the name of a great cause brings, to many people who see it, the analogy of the barbarity of the sacrifices that are now being made in the name of a god of war. Old fealties have crumbled away, and the individual human sacrifice has long since been discarded as belonging to an age of barbarism. When war and human sacrifice of the many have been banished, as that of the individual has been, eyes will be opened and ears unstopped, and men and women will understand all the wrongs of Society, and work together, nations with nations.

Address to the Woman's Peace Party
1916

At the outbreak of World War I in Europe, Lillian Wald and her closest associates, Jane Addams and Paul Kellogg, invited women and men of conscience to meet at Henry Street to discuss the government's "preparedness" campaign and emerging war hysteria. Academics, religious leaders, socialists, social workers, and members of the literary and theater world, the press, and the nursing profession were present.

From this meeting was formed an organization originally referred to as the Henry Street Group. As its aims became more clearly articulated its name changed, first to the American League for the Limitation of Armaments and then to the Anti-Preparedness Committee. Wald was opposed to such limited and negative-sounding names. In April 1916 the Anti-Preparedness Committee became the American Union Against Militarism (AUAM), with Wald as president.

In its first year the AUAM became a national clearinghouse of information and activity and one of the largest and most influential peace committees in the United States. The AUAM maintained a lobbyist in Washington and the only active nationwide press service for peace, and established local committees in twenty-two cities from Boston to San Francisco. The Union's statement of purpose demanded the prohibition of secret treaties, a ban on the private manufacture of war matériel and, to ensure "brakes on war," a national referendum to precede any declaration of war. They also campaigned to outlaw the more "atrocious weapons," and toured the countryside with a large model dinosaur to dramatize what happens when nations are too warlike.

AUAM member Emily Greene Balch, professor of Economics at Wellesley College, wrote that while war might engender "heroism and patriotism," in fact "the loss outweighs the gain. War makes fiends as well as heroes and ultimately demoralizes everyone."

Wald, in her official capacity as president of the AUAM, presented this speech on December 10, 1916, to the Woman's Peace Party of New York, which was headed by Crystal Eastman, a prominent feminist lawyer and executive secretary of the AUAM. Her reference to the Mexican crisis concerns a tangible AUAM success. Quick thinking and bold action on the part of Lillian Wald and her colleagues, notably Stanford University president David Starr Jordan, who represented the AUAM in El Paso, actually served to avert war with Mexico in 1916.

The creation of the American Union Against Militarism was, in the minds of the organizers, forced upon them. In the midst of the great war with ominous indications of a rising of the militarist spirit in America, the heavily endowed foundations for peace propaganda appeared to be uninterested in the phenomenon of existence of militaristic propaganda cloaked under the reasonable name of "preparedness."

The members of our organizing committee represented conservatism, Quakerism, socialism, the church, the press, literature, and social work. The unifying factor that brought us together was the sense of crisis [because] extraordinary and unprecedented measures had been taken to promote a public demand for military and naval expansion. [That] cost would not only be to the nation but to the world, since it seemed to us the sinister reversion to the war system would be at the cost of democracy.

The small group that directed this committee, and the enormous number of men and women who have affiliated themselves in one way or another with its propaganda, consider themselves true patriots of America,—patriotism that is borne of the passionate love for the best that is in America, not for rich America nor for successful America, but for the America of democracy, of ideals, and the America that stands for the things essential to a world of love and law and order.

A year ago at this time the evidences of hysteria in the "preparedness" campaign were as ridiculous in some instances as they were ominous for those who stand for the domination of civil authority as opposed to military control. The press was almost unanimous in giving expression to the sentiments of militarist propaganda. It laughed uproariously at the idealism of the Ford Peace Ship, but gave no evidence of its sense of humor as to some of the evidences of the other side. Boston women of standing were asked to register their automobiles, that the maidens might be carried inland when the Germans came. Solemn comment was everywhere made upon the women, who at the very beginning of the European war, bought blankets and placed them in cedar chests for our soldiers and more than a year ago one man who was "seeing things at night" declared in all seriousness that at two o'clock in the morning he *saw* a company of Germans drilling in Van Cortlandt Park of New York City. The officials of that great city held conferences and

I was present at one of them where it was intimated that strong guards should be immediately placed around the treasury in New York City. Germany, England, Canada, Japan, each in turn was pictured by some scared citizen as landing great armies on our shores, without warning or knowledge on our part, and carrying off our gold and our *maidens*.

The American Union Against Militarism considers itself an emergency committee, and during its year of existence has used all the money and brains that could be commanded to get sane consideration before the country. It sent a flying wedge of informed speakers to the West, hired great halls, addressed huge audiences, and laid the matter before the public to hear the "truth about the preparedness." Before the coming of the speakers "jingos" paraded the streets and even if our speakers failed to get on the front page the great dinosaur, symbolic of militarism, did appear there.

The Committee sent an ingenious and graphic exhibit, which was handled by the Woman's Peace Party, into the cities. The exhibitions were largely attended. In New York City from 5,000 to 10,000 people a day came to see it. They not only saw it, but gave evidence of seeing it thoughtfully. It was advertised as "The War Against War Exhibit."

Next came the Mexican crisis. At the time of the Carrizal incident the committee gathered together hurriedly, met until midnight, and the next morning paid for [full] page advertisements of Captain Morey's report of the incident. This was followed by an experiment in international publicity and direct action. Believing that the nearer war approached the more formidable it became, we summoned an unofficial joint conference to meet on the border and hold the peace. One Mexican and one American did actually get together at El Paso and the story gave further publicity and enlightenment to the country. Washington officials might tell of the result of this in the freely expressed opinions of thousands of American citizens upon our relationship to Mexico. The two men who met at El Paso later met in Washington and were joined by other representatives summoned by the American Union. A Mexican-American League was created to act in any future crisis. All of that may seem trifling but it anticipated the more important appointment of the Mexican-American Conference by the President of the

United States. Genuine opposition to war with Mexico became front page news and what is much better it became important news in Mexico—where word of our friendship reached the heart of Mexico and page-wide headlines filled the leading columns of some of the Spanish papers in that country.

The American Union Against Militarism believes that it has serious work before it this coming year. It is convinced of its obligation to create nationwide publicity . . . encourage delay on the entire shipbuilding program until the international agreement plans can be tried.

We plan to bring popular pressure to bear on Congress by deputations, public hearings, and the widest publicity in order to get the people to speak concerning the Army law which provides for conscription in case of war; to watch all attempts at militarist legislation, particularly the measures for universal military training. We want to cooperate with local peace societies in their efforts to keep military training out of the public schools; against conscription and compulsory military training in the state laws.

We are working in close affiliation with the Woman's Peace Party and we intend to continue our own peculiar methods, peculiar they are said to be for "pacifists." I am told that we are violating the popular conception of this group, and one newspaper which strongly disapproved of our aggressiveness against preparedness hysteria, said that, judging from our belligerency, we were the ones who "put the fist in pacifist." An editorial comment the other day discussed the demonstration of pacifists [as being] so much in earnest, they would fight for their conviction.

The Union believes that it should seriously and patiently construct the machinery for instant mobilization of the people for the prevention of any future war that might threaten this country. A war of simple wanton aggression against the United States is unthinkable. There would always be misunderstanding, false national pride, secret diplomacy, financial interests. At the base our plan for getting the people of the two countries into instant actual contact with an understanding of each other would always prevent this.

A year ago we began with one contributor and 15 members. We closed our year with a record of having spent $35,000 and with 6,000 members. . . . We have distributed some 600,000 pieces of literature of our own design and publication.

I should like to say that though we are against militarism we are not negative. We feel that we have been and are positive. Militarism is an evil growth which threatens our industrial democracy, our political institutions, our educational ideals and our international relationships. If the good things for which this country stands are to go on, clarion voices must ring out against movements that would destroy those precious possessions. The spirit of militarism has invaded us. It threatens the great constructive up-building, life-saving social work. To stamp it out, to recover the ground we have lost, to build upon them,—that is the task confronting all those who have the true interests of democracy at heart. We believe that militarism is opposed to democracy and that great numbers of citizens everywhere fear not so much an invading army but this other danger so close upon us—militarism. Good and true citizens of the great American Republic are united in this.

Sources

The speeches are from the Lillian Wald Papers, Rare Books and Manuscripts Division, The New York Public Library, Astor, Lenox, and Tilden Foundations (NYPL):

"Organization Amongst Working Women," *The Annals of the American Academy of Political and Social Science*, XXVII (May, 1906), 638–645. Box 34, Reel 24.

"Best Helps to the Immigrant Through the Nurse." Box 34, Reel 24.

Address to the House committee hearing on establishing a Federal Children's Bureau, Supplement to *The Annals of the American Academy of Political and Social Science* (March, 1909), 5–8. Box 34, Reel 24.

Address to a meeting under the auspices of the NAACP. Box 35, Reel 25.

"Suffrage." Box 35, Reel 25.

"New Aspects of Old Social Responsibilities." Box 35, Reel 25.

Address to the women's peace march organizing committee. Box 35, Reel 25.

"Women and War." Box 35, Reel 25.
Address to the Woman's Peace Party. Box 35, Reel 25.

Notes

1. Dock to Paul, September 4, 1914. Lillian D. Wald Papers, Rare Book and Manuscript Library, Columbia University, Box 5.
2. Peace Parade Committee to Wald. Columbia, Box 88.

Bibliography

Manuscript Collections

Adelaide Nutting Papers, Nursing Archives, Special Collections, Teachers College, Columbia University.

The Billy Rose Theatre Collection, The New York Public Library at Lincoln Center, Astor, Lenox, and Tilden Foundations.

Irene Lewisohn Library, Neighborhood Playhouse School of the Theatre.

Lillian D. Wald Papers, Rare Book and Manuscript Library, Columbia University Libraries.

Lillian Wald Papers, Rare Books and Manuscripts Division, The New York Public Library, Astor, Lenox, and Tilden Foundations.

Books and Articles

Addams, Jane. *Peace and Bread in Time of War*. New York: Garland Reprint, 1971 [1915].

———. *Twenty Years at Hull House*. Chautauqua, NY: The Chautauqua Press, 1911.

Birmingham, Stephen. *Our Crowd*. New York: Dell, 1967.

Cohen, Rose. *Out of the Shadow*. New York: Doran, 1918.

Cook, Blanche Wiesen. "Female Support Networks and Political Activisim: Lillian Wald, Crystal Eastman, Emma Goldman," in Linda Kerber and Jane De Hart-Mathews, eds., *Women's America, Refocusing the Past*, 2nd ed. New York: Oxford University Press, 1987.

———. "Woodrow Wilson and the Anti-Militarists, 1914–1917." Ph.D. diss. Johns Hopkins University, 1970.

———. ed. *Crystal Eastman: On Women and Revolution*. New York: Oxford University Press, 1978.

Crowley, Alice Lewisohn. *The Neighborhood Playhouse*. New York: Theatre Arts Books, 1959.

Daniels, Doris G. *Always A Sister: The Feminism of Lillian D. Wald*. New York: The Feminist Press, 1989.

Davis, Allen F. *American Heroine: The Life and Legend of Jane Addams*. New York: Oxford University Press, 1973.

———. *Spearheads for Reform*. New York: Oxford University Press, 1967.

Du Bois, W. E. B. *The Autobiography of W.E.B. Du Bois*. New York: International Publishers, 1968.

Duffus, R. L. *Lillian Wald: Neighbor and Crusader*. New York: Macmillian, 1938.

Goldman, Emma. *This Is My Story*. 2 vols. New York: Dover, 1970.

Goldmarck, Josephine. *Impatient Crusader: Florence Kelley's Life Story*. Urbana: University of Illinois Press, 1953.

Grimké, Angelina Weld. *Rachel*. College Park, MD: McGrath, 1969 [1920].

Hull, Gloria. *Color, Sex and Poetry: Three Women Writers of the Harlem Renaissance*. Indiana: Indiana University Press, 1987.

James, Janet, and Susan Reverby, eds. *A Lavinia Dock Reader*. New York: Garland, 1985.

Lagemann, Ellen. *A Generation of Women: Education in the Lives of Progressive Reformers*. Cambridge, MA: Harvard University Press, 1979.

Ovington, Mary White. *The Walls Came Tumbling Down*. New York: Schocken Books, 1970 [1947].

Reverby, Susan. *Ordered to Care: The Dilemma of American Nursing, 1850–1945*. New York: Cambridge University Press, 1987.

Siegel, Beatrice. *Lillian Wald of Henry Street*. New York: Macmillan, 1983.

Thoms, Adah H. *Pathfinders—A History of the Progress of Colored Graduate Nurses*, preface by Lillian D. Wald. New York: Garland Reprint, 1984 [1929].

Wald, Lillian D. *The House on Henry Street*. New York: Henry Holt, 1915.

———. *Windows on Henry Street*. Boston: Little, Brown, 1934.

———. "Development of Public Health Nursing in the United States." *The Trained Nurse and Hospital Review* (June 1928). Wald Papers, New York Public Library.

The Feminist Press at The City University of New York offers alternatives in education and in literature. Founded in 1970, this nonprofit, tax-exempt educational and publishing organization works to eliminate sexual stereotypes in books and schools and to provide literature with a broad vision of human potential. The publishing program includes reprints of important works by women, feminist biographies of women, and nonsexist children's books. Curricular materials, bibliographies, directories, and a quarterly journal provide information and support for students and teachers of women's studies. Through publications and projects, The Feminist Press contributes to the rediscovery of the history of women and the emergence of a more humane society.

New and Forthcoming Books

Always a Sister: The Feminism of Lillian D. Wald, a biography by Doris Groshen Daniels. $24.95 cloth.

Bamboo Shoots after the Rain: Contemporary Stories by Women Writers of Taiwan, 1945–1985, edited by Ann C. Carver and Sung-sheng Yvonne Chang. $29.95 cloth, $12.95 paper.

A Brighter Coming Day: A Frances Ellen Watkins Harper Reader, edited by Frances Smith Foster. $29.95 cloth, $13.95 paper.

The Daughters of Danaus, a novel by Mona Caird. Afterword by Margaret Morganroth Gullette. $29.95 cloth, $11.95 paper.

The End of This Day's Business, a novel by Katharine Burdekin. Afterword by Daphne Patai. $24.95 cloth, $8.95 paper.

Families in Flux (formerly *Household and Kin*), by Amy Swerdlow, Renate Bridenthal, Joan Kelly, and Phylllis Vine. $9.95 paper.

How I Wrote Jubilee *and Other Essays on Life and Literature*, by Margaret Walker. Edited by Maryemma Graham. $29.95 cloth, $9.95 paper.

Lone Voyagers: Academic Women in Coeducational Institutions, 1870–1937, edited by Geraldine J. Clifford. $29.95 cloth, $12.95 paper.

Not So Quiet: Stepdaughters of War, a novel by Helen Zenna Smith. Afterword by Jane Marcus. $26.95 cloth, $9.95 paper.

Seeds: Supporting Women's Work in the Third World, edited by Ann Leonard. Introduction by Adrienne Germain. Afterwords by Marguerite Berger, Vina Mazumdar, Kathleen Staudt, and Aminita Traore. $29.95 cloth, $12.95 paper.

Sister Gin, a novel by June Arnold. Afterword by Jane Marcus. $8.95 paper.

These Modern Women: Autobiographical Essays from the Twenties, edited and with a revised introduction by Elaine Showalter. $8.95 paper.

Truth Tales: Contemporary Stories by Women Writers of India, selected by Kali for Women. Introduction by Meena Alexander. $22.95 cloth, $8.95 paper.

We That Were Young, a novel by Irene Rathbone. Introduction by Lynn Knight. Afterword by Jane Marcus. $29.95 cloth, $10.95 paper.

What Did Miss Darrington See? An Anthology of Feminist Supernatural Fiction, edited by Jessica Amanda Salmonson. Introduction by Rosemary Jackson. $29.95 cloth, $10.95 paper.

Women Composers: The Lost Tradition Found, by Diane Peacock Jezic. $29.95 cloth, $12.95 paper.

For a free, complete backlist catalog, write to The Feminist Press at The City University of New York, 311 East 94 Street, New York, NY 10128. Send book orders to The Talman Company, Inc., 150 Fifth Avenue, New York, NY 10011. Please include $1.75 postage and handling for one book, $.75 for each additional.